To Olga,

May all of your travel clients say,
" I'll be back!"

Steg Hofner 2022

I'LL
BE
BACK

BOOKS BY SHEP HYKEN

Moments of Magic:
Be a Star with Your Customers and Keep Them Forever

The Loyal Customer: A Lesson from a Cab Driver

Only the Best on Success (coauthor)

Only the Best on Customer Service (coauthor)

Only the Best on Leadership (coauthor)

The Winning Spirit (coauthor)

Inspiring Others to Win (coauthor)

The Cult of the Customer: Create an Amazing Experience That Turns Satisfied Customers into Customer Evangelists

The Amazement Revolution: Seven Customer Service Strategies to Create an Amazing Customer (and Employee) Experience

Amaze Every Customer Every Time: 52 Tools for Delivering the Most Amazing Customer Service on the Planet

Be Amazing or Go Home: Seven Customer Service Habits That Create Confidence with Everyone

The Convenience Revolution: How to Deliver a Customer Service Experience That Disrupts the Competition and Creates Fierce Loyalty

SHEP HYKEN

I'LL
BE
BACK

HOW TO GET
CUSTOMERS TO COME
BACK AGAIN AND AGAIN

Published and distributed by:
SOUND WISDOM
P.O. Box 310
Shippensburg, PA 17257-0310
717-530-2122

info@soundwisdom.com

www.soundwisdom.com

Library of Congress Cataloging-in-Publication Data

Names: Hyken, Shep, author.

Title: I'll be back : how to get customers to come back again and again / Shep Hyken.

Description: Shippensburg, PA : Sound Wisdom, [2021]

Identifiers: LCCN 2020058240 | ISBN 9781640953017 (hardcover) | ISBN 9781640953024 (ebook)

Subjects: LCSH: Customer loyalty. | Customer services. | Consumer satisfaction.

Classification: LCC HF5415.525 .H94 2021 | DDC 658.8/342--dc23

LC record available at https://lccn.loc.gov/2020058240

ISBN 13 HC: 978-1-64095-301-7

ISBN 13 TP: 978-1-64095-310-9

ISBN 13 eBook: 978-1-64095-302-4

For Worldwide Distribution, Printed in the U.S.A.

1 2 3 4 5 6 7 8 / 25 24 23 22 21

CONTENTS

BUT WAIT...
THERE'S
MORE!

The REAL value of this book is online!

Go to **www.IllBeBackBook.com** to download the workbook and other bonus content!

And don't forget to follow me:

ShepHykenSpeaker ShepHyken @hyken ShepHyken @ShepHyken

WHAT WILL I LEARN FROM THIS BOOK?

PART 1 - THE BASICS OF CUSTOMER LOYALTY

Chapter 1: The Arnie

Question: What's the very best way to build a business that thrives during good times and bad? Answer: Win an Arnie, my special term for the experience you deliver that helps turn the people who buy from you into repeat customers – customers who think to themselves, or even say right out loud, "I'll be back." But here's the thing. Arnies don't happen by accident. We have to plan for them if we want to win them again and again.

This chapter addresses the following questions:

- How do you build a business that thrives during good times and bad?

- Is there a strategy that can set your company up for success, no matter what curveballs the world may throw your way?

- What are the three big ideas that will help you get the most from this book?

Chapter 2: The Most Important Measurement in Business

There are plenty of ways companies measure success and customer service. The famous NPS (Net Promoter Score) or CSAT (Customer Satisfaction) are two popular ones. But, all that data about how good you are doesn't mean anything if the customer doesn't come back. It's simple. Everyone must do the job they were hired to do, but they also have another responsibility – to make the customer want to come back!

This chapter addresses the following questions:

- What one trackable trend should leaders make sure they monitor every morning?

- What should we be measuring – happiness or behavior?

- Why do customers come back?

- Is a repeat customer the same as a loyal customer?

- How do you get customers to create a strong relationship with your company?

- How do you expand a relationship with a customer so that it's strong enough to sustain multiple renewals of trust?

Chapter 3: The Foundational Concepts

This is my take on Jan Carlzon's classic Moments of Truth concept about managing customer interactions. While he said they go one of two ways (good or bad), I believe they can go one of three ways: good, bad or average. I have names for these interactions. The bad ones are Moments of Misery™. The average ones are Moments of Mediocrity™. The good ones are Moments of Magic®.

This chapter addresses the following questions:

- What is a Moment of Truth?
- What is a Moment of Misery™?
- What is a Moment of Mediocrity™?
- What is a Moment of Magic®?
- What is Amazement?

Chapter 4: The Culture Challenge

Our employees will treat customers only as well as they themselves are treated. In this chapter, we look at the best ways to create and sustain a company culture that makes for loyal employees... and loyal customers. (This is for everybody.)

This chapter addresses the following questions:

- What is an "I'll Be Back" working culture?
- Why does an organization's culture matter?
- How does what happens inside the organization affect the customer experience?
- What core principles of a working culture make it easy for repeat customers to turn into loyal customers?

Chapter 5: Nothing Has Changed in Customer Service

It's not complicated. Nothing has really changed. The customer wants to be happy throughout their experience. When a customer has a problem, they let us know. We resolve it. That's the way it's always been and will always be. You might argue that there's a new way to do business using technology. While the way we go about it may have changed, the beginning and end of the customer's journey with us is still the same.

This chapter addresses the following questions:

- What is the essence of customer service?
- How has customer service changed?
- What do customers really want?
- What can we learn from unhappy customers?

PART 2 - MAKING LOYALTY A REALITY

Chapter 6: Want to Be Amazing? Just Be Better Than Average... All the Time!

Being amazing is within the grasp of every company and every person in the company. It doesn't mean you're always delivering over-the-top customer service. It means you're better than average – even just a little better than average – all of the time. It is a consistent and predictable experience that causes customers to use the word "always" before something positive that makes a company amazing. For example, "They always call me back quickly," or "They are always so helpful." A big one is, "Even when there is a problem, I know I can always count on them." A little better than average... Anyone can do it if they put their mind to it.

This chapter addresses the following questions:

- How do you change the way customers think about your company?
- What does amazement look like in practice?
- How do you get customers to rate you five out of five – and come back for more?
- What is the biggest obstacle to creating a consistently positive customer experience?

Chapter 7: The Shortest Customer Service Speech in History

If you gave me thirty seconds to deliver a great speech about customer service, I could pull it off and have about twenty-eight seconds to spare. The speech would go as follows: BE NICE! I could almost end this chapter there and it also would be the shortest chapter ever written on customer service – but in fact there is a lot to say about those two deceptively simple-sounding words. BE NICE is common sense that, unfortunately, may not be so common. In business, being nice is part of delivering customer service. It's the positive attitude, the respect you show the customer and the way you make them feel appreciated. It's an essential part of any customer service strategy. The best system isn't complete without the positive feelings the customer experiences from doing business with you.

This chapter addresses the following questions:

- What two simple words are the secret to a successful customer service program?

- What must you do to get customers to decide to do business with you again and again?

- What is the difference between a behavioral fit and a technical fit in a customer service position?

Chapter 8: How to Create Real Customer Loyalty

Customer loyalty is not about a lifetime. It's about the next time— every time. Don't confuse a repeat customer with a loyal customer. (That's the difference between a good marketing program and a true loyalty program.) Loyalty is about creating an emotional connection with the customer that makes price irrelevant and can bullet-proof you from your competition. (Or should I say, "terminator-proof" you from your competition?)

This chapter addresses the following questions:

- Why do most "loyalty programs" fail to create customer loyalty?

- What is the difference between a loyalty program and a marketing program?

- Why is "fine" a word you never want to hear from your customer?

- Where does true empathy for the customer start?

Chapter 9: Where Everybody Knows Your Name

What is personalization? Remember the 1980s sitcom *Cheers*? It was a popular sitcom that debuted in 1982 and remained popular for over ten years. The theme song, "Where Everybody Knows Your Name," was also the theme of the entire show. People like going to – and going back to – places where they are remembered. Start by using the customer's name. That's the root of a personalized experience. In this chapter, I'll show you how you can move on from there.

This chapter addresses the following questions:

- How do you make customers feel as if they are recognized and remembered and valued as individuals?

- Why does remembering a customer's name and history with your company have such a powerful effect on customer loyalty?

- How do you personalize the customer experience?

- What data can you leverage to make the customer feel at home?

Chapter 10: What Do You Stand For?

This is a major question with huge implications for creating and sustaining customer loyalty. Your company's values – including but not limited to the values that drive your community and charitable projects – are a powerful magnetizing force. They pull like-minded customers who share those values into your orbit. And once they're in that orbit, as long as you keep supporting the values, they'll keep wanting to do business with you... and keep referring other customers who feel the same way they do!

This chapter addresses the following questions:

- What is cause marketing and why does it have such a powerful effect on customer loyalty?
- Is cause marketing right for your organization?
- What goes into a successful cause marketing initiative?
- What companies have used cause marketing to create strong, enduring customer loyalty that serves as an advantage against competitors?

Chapter 11: Self-Service: Give the Customer Control... If It Creates a Better Experience

Some argue that self-service is not really customer service. But it is. In many cases, it's creating an easier and faster approach to getting problems resolved, researching information or making a purchase. Customers like taking control when it's easy, efficient and convenient. Don't miss out on giving your customers a good self-service opportunity.

This chapter addresses the following questions:

- When does offering a self-service option drive greater customer loyalty?
- What can you do to find new ways to let customers choose what happens next?
- Why is setting up and expanding self-service options a must, not an option?
- What are the six convenience principles?

Chapter 12: No Friction, Please

How easy is it to do business with your company? What can you do to make the experience of working with you smoother, more intuitive, and less of a hassle? When everything else is equal (that is, when there is a good product and good customer service), the company that is most convenient to do business with will win. Lower friction and eliminate anything that would get in the way of the customer saying, "They are so easy to do business with."

This chapter addresses the following questions:

- How can companies remove friction from the customer experience?
- What is the Friction Reduction Cycle?
- How do customer expectations about convenience affect purchase decisions – and customer loyalty?
- How do companies create friction for their customers without even realizing that's what they're doing?

Chapter 13: You Can't Automate a Relationship

In the digital age we're in, it's easy to let websites, chatbots and artificial intelligence take over. Don't become so enamored with the tech that you dehumanize the company. Very few companies have been able to create loyalty with a 100 percent digital platform. (Amazon and Zappos – now owned by Amazon – are two of the few.)

This chapter addresses the following questions:

- How can you build an emotional connection as part of your customer's experience?

- What is the Human Touch – and how can it affect customer loyalty if you never connect in person with the customer?
- What is a simple way to create an effective Human Touch program?
- How do some companies build an emotional connection with customers with little or no person-to-person contact?

Chapter 14: You're Terminated!

Why would a customer choose not to do business with you, or "terminate" the relationship? Here are the ten most likely reasons. Learn them! Make sure none of them impact your relationship with a given customer! And if, for some reason, you decide it is time to "terminate" a relationship with a customer, here's how you do it without causing problems down the line.

This chapter addresses the following questions:

- What are the most likely reasons for a customer to decide to stop doing business with you?
- How can you keep customers from ending their relationship with your company?
- When does it make sense to cut ties with a customer – and how should you do that?

Chapter 15: Where the Rubber Meets the Road

Now that I've shared the most important principles that connect to creating and sustaining customer loyalty, you're ready to make it happen in your organization. This chapter gives you a six-step process you can use to develop specific customer loyalty initiatives that will fit perfectly in your world.

This chapter addresses the following questions:

- What is the process for creating an experience that customers choose to come back to again and again?
- How long is this process likely to take?
- Who should be involved in it?
- Why is knowing what your competition does only the beginning, not the end, of the discussion?

Epilogue: I Want You to Come Back

My closing words and comments. I don't want this book to be a one-time read. I want it to be a guide that brings the reader back again and again. In other words, I want the reader to say, "I'll be back."

The epilogue wraps up the entire book and addresses the following questions:

- How do you start a loyalty revolution?
- How do you build internal alliances that will help you to launch and sustain that revolution?

PART 1

THE BASICS OF CUSTOMER LOYALTY

In this part of the book, you will learn why customer loyalty is so important and why a repeat customer is not necessarily a loyal customer. You will also get an overview of the core principles that make customer loyalty possible.

THE ARNIE

Question: What's the best way to build a business that thrives during good times and bad?

Answer: Win an Arnie.

At this point, you're probably asking yourself: *What's an Arnie? I've never heard of that.* Well, you're right. You haven't. And there's a reason you haven't heard of it before. An "Arnie" is a special term for the experience you deliver that helps turn the people who buy from you into *repeat customers* – customers who think to themselves, or even say right out loud, "I'll be back."

> ## Arnies don't happen by accident. We have to plan for them if we want to win them.

But here's the thing. An Arnie is not an award given out once a year to a few elite people. It happens every day, all the time, whenever customers make that critical decision that they want to keep doing business with a company. It's a moment that has to be earned over and over again.

Up to this point, you may not have considered the possibility that a successful business strategy could be built around Hollywood legend and former governor of California Arnold Schwarzenegger's most famous tagline. But Arnold's best-known line, "I'll be back," points us toward a vitally important principle when it comes to creating and sustaining a competitive edge in the marketplace: *Repeat business, and especially business that results from customer loyalty, makes all the difference.* Those three words, "I'll be back," are game changers. This book is about generating them more often, more strategically, and more reliably than your competition. What we are striving for is a customer who thinks and says, "I'll be back... always!" The question is: How do we get there?

The more moments you can deliver that support, encourage and reinforce the "I'll be back" response, the better off your business will be... and the greater the likelihood that it will survive and thrive, no matter what curveballs the marketplace, the global economy, or the world at large may throw your way.

So, whether you deal directly with customers, you lead a team that does, or you are a leader who wants to build a better customer experience into the organizational DNA of your company, you have come to the right place. If you are intrigued by the possibility of getting large numbers of your customers to say, "I'll be back," you've come to the right place. And if you're an entrepreneur looking to build your business around the idea of attracting and retaining loyal customers, you've come to the right place. If you fall into any of those categories, this book is for you.

Before we get started in earnest, let me share three simple ideas with you that will help you to get the most out of this book.

BIG IDEA #1:
SET YOURSELF APART...
BY OPENING YOUR MIND

> *"What is the point of being on this Earth if you are going to be like everyone else?"*
>
> Arnold Schwarzenegger[1]

Some of what I'll be sharing with you in these pages falls into the category of "common sense." (When it comes to customer service, common sense isn't always that common!) You may have read or heard about a few of these ideas before or be practicing some of them already. That's great! However, some of what I'll be sharing with you in this book will probably feel a little unfamiliar to you. Certain concepts and strategies may even challenge your paradigm and take you out of your comfort zone. Embrace that. Don't let force of habit keep you from trying something new, something that could help you take your team and your organization to the next level. By keeping an open mind, by doing things you haven't done before, you can begin the process of positioning your product or service as something unique and irreplaceable in your customer's world. You will set yourself apart in a positive way. That's a good thing!

BIG IDEA #2:
BE WILLING TO
CHANGE YOUR PROCESSES

"If you don't find the time, if you don't do the work, you don't get the results."

Arnold Schwarzenegger[2]

If you've made it this far in the book, I'm assuming you agree that building your business around the principle of customer loyalty is a sound strategic decision. You should know that it's also something that requires sustained effort, flexibility, and the willingness to create and execute entirely new processes. This will take time, effort, commitment, and coalition-building. Make those investments. You won't regret doing so, I promise.

BIG IDEA #3:
TAKE ACTION

"You can't climb the ladder of success with your hands in your pockets."

Arnold Schwarzenegger[3]

At the end of each chapter, you will find Key Points, Conversation Starters, and one or more action items listed under Take Action. Use them! Don't just read the ideas and strategies for enhancing customer loyalty, do something with them! Discuss them with your colleagues. The only way this book can have a positive impact on you and your team is if you make a habit, chapter by chapter, of acting on what you have learned.

ONE MORE THING

The principles in this book are timeless and relevant to all industries. They can be, and have been, implemented successfully at companies large and small. Occasionally, I'll offer case studies or examples to illustrate a certain point. Don't get distracted by the differences between the specific businesses I mention and *your* business. Focus on the commonalities and on the key lessons that the stories convey. On a similar note, please don't be distracted by the word "customer" if that is not what you call the person who buys your products and/or services. I use the word "customer" as an all-purpose identifier. Everything I share about "customers" is equally relevant to any of the people your organization serves: clients, guests, members, patients, visitors, residents, you name it.

> For the purposes of this book, a customer is anyone who does business with you.

Here is the bottom line: The very best way to secure sustained growth for your business over time is to increase the number of *repeat customers* you serve and to turn as many of those repeat customers as possible into loyal customers.

Perhaps you're wondering if a loyal customer is the same as a repeat customer. Maybe you're wondering how you can create and maintain customer loyalty.

These are some of the big questions that we'll be examining together in the chapters that follow.

Let's get started. But before we do – here's one last insight from Arnold:

> *"Be hungry for success, hungry to make your mark, hungry to be seen and to be heard, hungry to have an effect. And as you move up and become successful, be sure also to be hungry for helping others."*
>
> Arnold Schwarzenegger[4]

In the next chapter, we'll examine the most overlooked metric in business today.

KEY POINTS

- The three magic words in customer service are "I'll be back."
- The best way to secure a sustainable growth position for your business over time is to increase the number of repeat customers you serve and to turn as many

of those repeat customers as possible into loyal customers.

- The more moments there are that support, encourage, and reinforce the "I'll be back" response, the better off your business will be... and the greater the likelihood that it will survive and thrive.

- Building your business around the principle of customer loyalty requires sustained effort, flexibility, and the willingness to create and execute entirely new processes.

- This book will take you out of your comfort zone. Embrace that.

- The only way this book can have a positive impact on you and your team is if you make a habit, chapter by chapter, of acting on what you have learned.

CONVERSATION STARTERS

- On a scale of 1 to 10, how willing are you to try something new when it comes to interacting with your customers?

- What processes would your best customers most like to see changed?

- What actions have you already taken to learn more about your best customers? What further actions could you take?

TAKE ACTION!

Keep reading! Move on to Chapter 2!

NOTES

1. Source: *I Wasn't There to Compete. I Was There to Win: 110 Pages Notebook with Motivational Quote* by Arnold Schwarzenegger, Score Your Goal Publications, 2019.

2. Source: *The New Encyclopedia of Modern Bodybuilding: The Bible of Bodybuilding*, Arnold Schwarzenegger, Simon & Schuster, 1999.

3. Source: "Six Rules on How to Be Successful," speech at the University of Southern California, www.graduationwisdom.com. May 15, 2009.

4. Source: *I Wasn't There to Compete. I Was There to Win: 110 Pages Notebook with Motivational Quote* by Arnold Schwarzenegger, Score Your Goal Publications, 2019.

CHAPTER 2

THE MOST IMPORTANT MEASUREMENT IN BUSINESS

What would you say is the single most important measurement in the world of business?

What one metric matters most? What one trackable trend should leaders make absolutely sure is showing up on their dashboard every morning? What number should they always monitor closely?

You are likely to hear a lot of different answers to this important question. These answers come from a wide variety of authorities, each with their own perspective. Of course, sales numbers, revenue, profit, and expenses are all important. However, the measurement that each and every business leader should be watching like a hawk is this one: *Does the customer come back?*

This is the most unjustly overlooked metric in the business world today. There are a lot of metrics related to customer service and experience for business leaders to choose from, of course. Let's take a moment to consider the ones that are most likely to enter this discussion.

Two of the most popular metrics are the Net Promoter Score (NPS) and the Customer Satisfaction Score (CSAT). NPS measures how likely someone is to recommend a business to someone else. CSAT measures the level of satisfaction the customer experiences with a given product, service, or interaction with a brand. Both of these focus on a customer's happiness with the business, product, service, or interaction.

A third metric, the Customer Effort Score (CES), also focuses on happiness, but it does so indirectly, by focusing on the level of effort someone is willing to make in order to interact with a business's products and services. CES typically is measured immediately after a person connects with customer support, and the surveys that generate this metric are often, but not always, conducted right after a purchase decision. Basically, CES measures how easy a business is to work with, and it helps to throw a spotlight on areas of the process that could be improved to make the customer a little happier. Think of CES as identifying potential *obstacles* to happiness. These surveys are rising in popularity because research shows[1] that consumers who describe "low effort" to engage with a business are likely to come back.

By the way, a brief word is probably in order here on the topic of convenience as a competitive advantage in your relationship with the customer. This is a massive subject, one that's covered in depth in my book *The Convenience Revolution*. I deal with current issues connected to self-service and the reduction of customer experience friction in Chapters 11 and 12 of this book, because these are essential topics for anyone putting together a comprehensive loyalty strategy. But for an extensive review of the subject, please read *The Convenience Revolution*.

HAPPINESS OR BEHAVIOR?

A question I often hear from business leaders is, "Of the three (NPS, CSAT, and CES), which is most important?" They're all important. I like them all. Each of these metrics has its place. But what I want you to notice is that these metrics measure happiness, which is very important, but not behavior. There's a big difference.

CSAT surveys tell us how satisfied customers are (or at least how satisfied they say they are), but winning a high score does not necessarily translate into the behavior we want: repeat business from the customer. It's also worth noticing that the word "satisfied" can mean very different things to different people, so a certain amount of subjectivity is baked into every CSAT survey. Last, but not least, the customer's response may be heavily influenced by factors we can't understand or control (like what kind of day the person taking the survey is having, and how stressed he or she is as a result).

NPS surveys give us great, important information about how likely people are to recommend us. But to generate a better understanding and meaningful results, they require follow-up. While the NPS question helps us understand whether customers are happy (or unhappy), we don't know *why* they feel the way they feel. This sometimes leads to a "tunnel vision" effect where we miss out on important shifts in attitude and aspirations. This is why follow-up questions are important – for this and many other types of surveys. Moreover, the answers people give us about whether they would recommend us don't actually measure *behavior*, either from the person we're talking to or from anyone else in their circle.

CES surveys provide invaluable insights about which parts of the process are working – and which aren't. Because they are usually conducted immediately after an interaction, when people are less likely to devote much time to answering the questions, these surveys often don't tell us a whole lot about *whom* we've just been talking to. We may not know what *kind* of customer is answering our questions. Not only that, but the people responding to these surveys may end up giving us low grades for the amount of "effort" required to do something that really doesn't match up with our business plan. For instance, we can get a low CES score because the person was looking for, and failed to find, a certain product on our website – a product we have never offered and do not plan to offer. Finally, CES surveys, like the other two metrics I've mentioned, track how people *feel* – not what they actually *do*.

How customers feel is important, of course. But I believe we should also look closely at what percentage of our customer base *makes a repeat purchase from us over a given time period*. At the end of the day, this is the measurement that really matters.

We know that this number connects to a decision to do business with us again. That's the definition of the metric. It also gives us statistically meaningful data about how we're doing in the marketplace. And by looking at which products and service are (or aren't) attracting repeat customers, we can get a clearer picture of what is making customers happy (or unhappy). Not only that, this repeat-customer number can be easily traced to customers who have taken action on specific product/service offerings. We can identify which customers have *actually made* a repeat purchase... and what they decided to buy from us! We can use this metric to focus on the behavior.

Please understand, I'm not saying that CSAT, NPS, or CES are unimportant. I'm not saying we shouldn't track them (and other metrics), or that they don't share important lessons, or that we shouldn't notice what direction these metrics are headed. All I'm saying is that the metric that should be at the top of our list of priorities, the one that can have the biggest impact on our business, is whether customers *actually come back!*

All the other measurements determine whether the customer is happy with us. We should stop and ask ourselves: *Why are we interested in that?* Because happiness is supposed to be an *indicator* of whether they will buy from us again!

Regardless of how happy our customers are, we need to know *with certainty* whether they are actually coming back to buy from us again... how often they are doing that... and what they are choosing to buy when they do.

A customer who comes back to us is, by definition, a customer we have not lost. This decision to buy from us again is a victory in our ongoing war against high rates of customer churn. Of course, that victory is much more meaningful if the decision to buy from us is rooted in a decision based on a strong *emotional tie* between us and the customer.

WHY DO CUSTOMERS COME BACK?

Let's face it, some customers come back because of reasons other than loyalty. They may simply be buying on price, or on location, or because of some other factor that has nothing to do with any relationship that's been built up over time. The minute someone else shows up with a lower price or a more convenient location, that competitor may get the business. The question isn't just whether we hold on to the customer. It's whether we hold on to the customer in such a way that there is a powerful *relationship* in place, one that serves as a barrier to competitors who want to take the customer away.

The stakes are high. Whenever we lose a customer to the competition, there is not just the loss of that customer's business, which includes an immediate loss of revenue, but also the loss of that customer's recurring business. And let's not forget about the potential loss of referrals to other customers.

Consider, too, that customer churn does not just mean the loss of revenue and referrals. It also includes the major cost of trying to acquire new customers to replace those we have lost! Unfortunately, many companies focus far more on customer acquisition than they do on customer retention… despite the fact that, according to a 2018 study,[2] it costs five times more to attract a new customer than to retain a current one.

We must measure, consistently and accurately, how well we are doing at persuading customers to come back and buy from us again. When this number is headed in the right direction, based on a *strong investment in an ongoing relationship* with us, we win. When it is headed in the wrong direction, when people don't choose to stay with us because of the relationship, we lose.

MORE THAN A RECEIPT

Let me give you a concrete example of what I mean when I talk about a *strong investment in an ongoing relationship* with a company.

I used to buy all my business suits from one particular store. I had been buying from that store – we'll call them Store A – for over twenty years. I was happy with Store A. How do we *know* I was happy with them? I kept going back to them to buy suits.

For me, buying business suits is an incredibly important purchase decision because I'm a professional speaker. When I step onto the stage, the clothes I wear make an important statement about my business, about my brand, and about me as a person. The suit I choose to wear when addressing an audience has to be stylish, but not cutting-edge stylish. It has to be professional, not groundbreaking, and it has to send the silent message of *authority*. Suffice to say, buying a suit is a pretty big deal for me. And for years, the way I handled this important purchasing decision was to go to that same store – specifically, the same salesman who had been taking care of me for all those years.

Then came the fateful day when I had a problem with something I'd bought from Store A. I talked to them about it, and I wasn't satisfied with the way the problem was resolved. I won't bother you with all the details of the problem here; I'll just say it had to do with whether a shirt I had bought was the size that I had ordered. (Spoiler alert: It wasn't.)

They seemed to disagree with me. I was surprised that there was even a discussion about it. My normal salesman at this store would never have disagreed. Unfortunately, that person had moved on. I no longer had "someone on the inside" at Store A. Notice that I didn't *complain* about this personnel change to anyone. But it was an issue. Why? Because sometimes the customers who *aren't* complaining are the ones you need to focus on. Sometimes, the people who say *fine* really aren't fine. Sometimes these supposedly satisfied customers become opportunities for the competition!

Enter Matti.

Matti works at a competing store that I'll call Store B. Every once in a while, I bought ties or other accessories there. Not long ago, I was in that store, looking at ties, and Matti, who had never helped me pick out a suit before, smiled and said, "Shep, why don't you buy your business suits here?"

Great question! I told Matti that I'd been buying suits from the other store for years. I mentioned that "someone on the inside" at Store A had helped me make good decisions and that this person had since moved on.

Matti *listened* to everything I had to say. Then she said, "I'll tell you what. Why don't you buy one suit from me? I'll show you how I work. And I'll bet you that, based on the very first suit you buy from me, you will never want to buy a suit anywhere else." Notice that Matti wasn't just trying to sell a single suit. She was thinking about the next time. She was focused on earning, building, and renewing trust with me.

I liked her style, and perhaps most importantly, whether I was conscious of it or not, I liked her commitment to building an *ongoing* personal relationship with me as her customer. So I told Matti that I would buy my next suit from her... and together we would see what happened next.

Matti did not disappoint. She asked me all kinds of questions about my business, about the kinds of groups I talked to, about the decision makers I typically dealt with. She asked me what kinds of suits I had bought in the past. And she asked me what specific events I was looking forward to in the immediate future.

Matti was totally committed to making sure that I looked great in front of my audience. Before she made a recommendation, she even visited my home, took a look at the suits in my closet, and got a firsthand sense of what had worked for me in the past in terms of suit selection.

Not only did Matti suggest a great suit for me, she positioned herself as a *partner* in my world, someone who had a personal stake in my success. All of a sudden, I had "someone on the inside" again, someone who was looking out for me.

Matti created a loyal customer with the effort and care she took in helping me look my best. She created that emotional connection that drives both repeat business and coveted customer loyalty. As a result, I don't just have a *receipt* from Matti's store, I now have a *relationship* with Matti's store.

Customer loyalty is a strong personal investment in a relationship with the company.

THE ART OF RENEWING

Matti understood something important:

The customer relationship is more important than the individual purchase.

She thought not in terms of transactions, but in terms of building a relationship that is strong enough to sustain multiple renewals of trust.

The word *renewal* is important. Most people think that a renewal applies to some type of subscription. You renew your subscription to a magazine, a maintenance contract, or a software program. But what if the word renewal had a broader meaning?

What if renewal simply meant that the customer had a strong enough emotional connection with you to come back—again and again? While repeat business may not be as steady as an automatic monthly or annual subscription renewal, it can still be tracked in a similar way. A business with a true subscription model can predict renewals. Over time, any business can track return customers who are renewing their trust in the business to purchase from them again and again.

Let's broaden the whole idea of subscription. Typically, a subscription means ongoing and recurring revenue to a company from customers paying on a schedule—monthly, quarterly, or yearly. It can utilize something as simple as a subscription card or a formal legal contract that binds the customer for a certain amount of time. Either way, it's an agreement that says, "I'll pay you for ongoing products or services until the subscription runs out or I stop renewing."

When you take away the formality of the subscription arrangement, you have business as usual. The customer is not under any obligation or agreement to keep doing business with you. You must prove your value to get them to come back. You must renew the trust they have placed in you. When you do, they will renew their commitment to buy from you again. Customers renewing their relationship with you by coming back to buy again and again are proof of your renewing and deepening their trust in working with you.

I can't think of any business that wouldn't want their customers to come back. Doesn't yours? And isn't that renewal rate worth measuring?

Our goal, like Matti's goal, must always be to *focus on the next time*. Loyalty is not about a lifetime. It's about the next time, every time. What are you doing *today* to get the customer to come back next time? How can you advance the relationship? How can you manage the customer's experience so that it deepens trust... and increases the likelihood of the customer returning to buy from you again?

WHAT IS YOUR RENEWAL STRATEGY?

Your strategy must be unique to your business and your customers, but I can tell you this much: It must be based on creating value and building trust in the relationship.

Identifying and executing your business's renewal strategy is the critical challenge we will be addressing throughout this book. My goal is to help you identify the best ways to set, plan for, and execute a powerful renewal strategy – no matter what you and your company sell.

In the next chapter, we'll look at some foundational concepts that will help you to get the most out of this book.

KEY POINTS

- Measurement and feedback are important, but the measurement that matters most is how often customers come back.

- When customers come back, based on a strong investment in an ongoing relationship with us, we win. When they don't, we lose.

- When customers continue their relationship with us by coming back to buy again and again, that means we have *renewed* and deepened their trust in doing business with us.

- The customer relationship is more important than the individual purchase.

- Our goal to build customer loyalty must always be to focus on the next time, every time – by creating value and building trust.

CONVERSATION STARTERS

- What measurements do you use right now to understand your business?

- What could you be measuring that you aren't measuring right now?

- What do the numbers tell you? What could they be telling you?

- What action will you take, based on your assessment of the numbers?

TAKE ACTION!

Talk to your most reliable repeat customers and find out what made them decide to do business with you again. Was there a specific incident? A series of events? After the conversation, review your notes and identify the value you deliver to your best customers.

NOTES

1. Dixon, Freeman, and Toman, "Stop Trying to Delight Your Customers," *Harvard Business Review,* July/August 2010. https://hbr.org/2010/07/stop-trying-to-delight-your-customers.

2. Source: "Acquisition vs Retention: The Importance of Customer Lifetime Value" https://www.huify.com/blog/acquisition-vs-retention-customer-lifetime-value.

CHAPTER 3

THE FOUNDATIONAL CONCEPTS

Here's a big question for you.

When should we start working on getting the customer to come back—to renew their "subscription"?

The first time they choose to do business with us, of course. That's what Matti was doing. That's what this book is really all about: finding more effective ways to focus on the next time, right now. That's the big idea here.

At this point, I need to share some important concepts that support that big idea. The ideas you're about to encounter have been an integral part of all the books that I've written and just about all of my speeches, and if you've followed my work for any period of time, you should recognize them immediately. If you're new to these concepts, please review what follows carefully. If you're *not* new to these concepts, please review them *even more carefully* than you did the first time. What follows is a very brief, but essential refresher course in the foundational concepts that support the goal of *focusing on the next time* with the customer. In my experience, the willingness to *reinforce* these ideas is a key predictor of success.

Whether you are already familiar with the ideas I'll be sharing with you in this chapter or have never encountered them before, please take the time to reinforce them by reading the chapter carefully. Ask yourself: *How does this apply to our organization?*

KEY CONCEPT: MOMENT OF TRUTH

A Moment of Truth is a term coined by Jan Carlzon, the former president of Scandinavian Airlines. He defined the Moment of Truth in business as... "any time the customer comes into contact with any aspect of a business, however remote, and has an opportunity to form an impression." It's important to remember that Moments of Truth can be good, bad, or average. I use three special terms to describe those three possible Moments of Truth: Moments of Misery™, Moments of Mediocrity™, and Moments of Magic®.

KEY CONCEPT: MOMENT OF MISERY™

A Moment of Misery is a negative interaction. It's a problem, a complaint, a clunky process, or even a bad attitude from an employee. It's what I experienced when I got the wrong size shirt and couldn't get a replacement for it from Store A. My guess is that you've experienced plenty of Moments of Misery in the past. One common example of a Moment of Misery can occur when being transferred to different departments during a phone call to a company help line. The customer has to repeatedly explain their problem because the customer service representative transferring them can't be bothered to stay on the line and explain things to the next representative. Moments of Misery come in all shapes and sizes, and they can involve digital interactions as well as face-to-face or voice-to-voice conversations.

KEY CONCEPT: MOMENT OF MEDIOCRITY™

As the name suggests, a Moment of Mediocrity is an average or mediocre service experience. It doesn't stand out. It's not positive. It's not negative. It might even be considered satisfactory. It may meet our expectations, but there's nothing special about it. It happens when someone does the job to minimum standards. It does nothing to advance the relationship. Again, we've all experienced this. Think of the last time you dealt with somebody who did only what was absolutely necessary, no more and no less. Maybe they had an apathetic attitude, created a feeling that work was "inconvenient," or they were obviously bored with their job. That was a Moment of Mediocrity. While it was nothing to complain about, it was nothing to write home about, either. People describe the experience as okay, satisfactory, or fine. These can happen in person, on a phone call, or digitally via text message, video call, email, or some other online platform.

KEY CONCEPT: MOMENT OF MAGIC®

A Moment of Magic is a positive experience or interaction with someone or some company serving you. As you might imagine, these also come in many different forms—person to person, voice to voice and digital. Sometimes, people get distracted by the word "magic" here. Please understand that magic doesn't necessarily mean a "WOW" or incredible, over-the-top level of service—although it could. In most cases, a Moment of Magic is just an above-average experience. Sometimes it's only a little bit better than average or satisfactory; other times, it's memorable, something that is truly special. Usually, though, a Moment of Magic is the slightly-above-average way that a company or an individual handles the interaction. For example, you are impressed when someone from the company returns a call or email in a short period of time. It doesn't sound all that special, but it's still a positive, above-average experience. Occasionally, these moments come from Moments of Misery that are handled well. In fact, that's where those memorable WOW experiences so often come from: problems or complaints that are properly resolved in a way that impresses the customer.

It's been said that a complaint is a gift from your customer. These "gifts" are opportunities to fix a problem and show the customer how good you are. If Store A (the men's clothing store we covered in Chapter 2) had properly followed up on my complaint about the shirt that didn't quite fit, they would have turned my Moment of Misery into a Moment of Magic, helping to protect themselves from the competitor that eventually took away their customer.

Every Moment of Truth, even if it's a Moment of Misery, is the opportunity to create a Moment of Magic!

KEY CONCEPT: AMAZEMENT

Sometimes people hear the word "amazement" and think of companies that somehow manage to deliver truly mind-blowing levels of customer service, time and time again. That's no easy feat. In fact, it may be close to impossible. I have a different definition of what "amazement" means, one that puts amazement within reach of everyone. Amazement is simply a predictable and consistent above-average experience received by the customer. It happens when there is a predictable sequence of Moments of Magic that is consistent enough to inspire confidence in our customers.

By now, you have the idea. There are countless Moments of Truth, which mean countless opportunities to manage the interactions with customers that can become Moments of Magic. If we string together enough Moments of Magic, we deliver amazement. It's easier than we may think to identify ways to turn an average moment into something just a little bit better. Very often, it doesn't cost anything to do this! Sometimes, it's just a smile. Sometimes, it's saying "Good morning" or "Good afternoon." Sometimes, it's smiling and asking a question like, "Shep, why don't you buy your business suits here?" – and really listening to the answer.

In the next chapter, we'll look at one of the critical factors that makes amazement possible, both inside and outside the organization: culture.

KEY POINTS

- The phrase "Moment of Truth" is a term coined by Jan Carlzon, the former president of Scandinavian Airlines. Carlzon defined[1] the Moment of Truth as: "any time the customer comes into contact with any aspect of a business, however remote, and has an opportunity to form an impression."

- A Moment of Misery™ is a negative interaction. It's a problem, a complaint, a clunky process, or even a bad attitude from an employee.

- A Moment of Mediocrity™ is an average or mediocre experience. It doesn't stand out. It's not negative—nothing to complain about. And it's definitely not positive—nothing to write home about. At best, it's average or satisfactory.

- A Moment of Magic® is a positive experience or interaction. Typically, it's just a little above average. Sometimes, it can be an over-the-top experience.

- Every Moment of Truth, even if it is a Moment of Misery, is an opportunity to create a Moment of Magic.

- Amazement happens when there are predictable Moments of Magic (above-average experiences) consistently enough to inspire confidence in our customers so they want to do business with us again... because they know what to expect and they like it!

CONVERSATION STARTERS

- When was the last time you, as a customer, experienced a Moment of Misery, and the company turned it into a Moment of Magic? How did they do that? How did that make you feel about the company?

- When was the last time you, as a customer, experienced a Moment of Misery that *didn't* turn into a Moment of Magic? How did that make you feel?

- What does a Moment of Magic look like for your customer? Give a couple of examples.

- Think about a specific time when your company created a Moment of Misery and turned it into a Moment of Magic. How did that happen? How could you make that kind of moment happen again?

TAKE ACTION!

Notice the next Moment of Magic you create for a customer. Then share what happened with your team members.

NOTE

1. Carlzon, Jan. *Moments of Truth: New Strategies for Today's Customer-Driven Economy.* Harper Business, 2001 (Revised edition).

CHAPTER 4

THE CULTURE CHALLENGE

Think for a moment about someone who just became a smiling first-time customer of yours, someone who says to friends and family, "I really love doing business with them."

That's what you want the person to say, right? It's a great outcome. You should be proud of that! That kind of response sets up repeat business with that person, which in turn sets up the possibility of long-term loyalty. Of course, you love hearing that. Yet there is a question to consider, an important one.

In that one beautiful sentence, "I really love doing business with them" – who is *them?*

Remember, this is a first-time customer. In all likelihood, they haven't interacted with many people on your team. The odds are pretty good, in fact, that they've interacted with only *one* person. That is worth noticing. Based on an interaction with *one* person, the customer has made a generalization about your *entire* organization.

Isn't that remarkable? One good interaction between a couple of people, and now the customer is out there telling *everyone* that they really love doing business with the *whole* company.

It works in the other direction as well.

Let's say that, tomorrow, somebody on your team is giving customers less than their best, for whatever reason... and nineteen other team members are having great days, doing a superb job and making all kinds of Moments of Magic happen. But that first-time customer happens to run into the one employee who's not hitting the mark.

What do you think *that* customer is going to say to friends and family about your organization?

"I really hate doing business with *them*."

Even though nineteen team members were doing a great job, the twentieth one was the team member who defined the word "*them*" for the customer!

IMPRESSION IS REALITY

Why do I share these examples with you? Simple.

If our goal is to create long-term loyalty with individual customers, we want the odds on our side. That means we want to make sure that *everyone* in the organization is on board, *everyone* is in the right role, *everyone* is tuned into what we're doing as an organization and why we're doing it, and *everyone* is motivated to amaze.

Call it the "I'll Be Back" working culture.

Here is the key point: Each employee, at every level of the organization, needs to understand and buy into this kind of working culture. I'm not just talking about frontline people who interact with customers. I'm talking about the *entire* organization. I've covered this topic in other books, but it's too important not to address in this one, because making meaningful improvements in customer loyalty is simply impossible if the working culture is out of whack. So, what follows is a very brief overview of what goes into building and supporting that kind of culture. I realize that I'm only scratching the surface of the subject with what follows. I could easily write a whole book on this topic, and perhaps someday I will. But I'm including the following because *everyone* in the organization needs to know the basics, and everyone in the organization can benefit from understanding a leader's perspective on these issues.

> At the end of the day, customer service is not a department, but a philosophy to be embraced by everyone in an organization. It's part of the culture of a company.

Now, I realize that not all companies are identical and no two working cultures are exactly the same. But I stand by the principle that every organization that is serious about loyalty must develop an "I'll Be Back" working culture. And yes, even though workplaces differ, there is one thing that all of the "I'll Be Back" working cultures I have helped to set up *always* have in common: *Everyone Has to Be in It to Win It!*

PRINCIPLE #1:
EVERYONE HAS TO BE IN IT TO WIN IT!

When you're part of a company where the working culture embraces the principle that *Everyone Has to Be in It to Win It*, it doesn't matter whether you're the CEO, a shipping clerk, a salesperson, a warehouse worker, an accountant, or someone interacting directly with the customer in real time – you know that *your* contribution impacts what happens to the customer experience whether you actually see the customer or not.

Let's say you're an accountant. If the invoice you set up has the wrong total on it, does that impact the customer experience? Does that error have any effect on whether they are inspired to say, "I love working with them"? You bet. At best, it causes the customer to be frustrated when they find the error. At worst, it causes a lack of confidence.

How about if you're working in the warehouse, and you lose track of what you're doing for a moment, and you ship the customer the wrong item? Is that going to have an impact on the customer? Of course it will.

And of course, if you're the CEO (or any other senior-level leader), practically every decision you make and every action you take is going to have some impact on the customer experience. If the customer experience isn't your "North Star," the point in the sky by which you navigate the team and the company, it should be.

Here's the reality: When an organization's working culture is built around the idea that *everyone* has a hand in determining the quality of the experience the customer has, and *everyone* has a stake in delivering Moments of Magic, customers notice. Not only do customers notice, they tell their friends and family.

I've just shared one critical element of the "I'll Be Back" working culture: Delivering amazement is about *you*, no matter what your job title is. However far back in the company you might be from the standpoint of connecting with the outside customer, you have your role, and it affects the customer experience. If you don't do what you're supposed to do, it is going to be felt, eventually, on the outside.

Here are five more pieces of the "I'll Be Back" puzzle.

PRINCIPLE #2:
FOLLOW THE EMPLOYEE GOLDEN RULE

The way we want our customers to be treated must be congruent with the way people are treated internally. I call this idea the Employee Golden Rule: Do unto employees as you want done unto the customer – maybe even better.

There is no wiggle room here. The culture of your organization must be one that celebrates, values, and supports employees. If it doesn't do those things, customers will not feel celebrated, valued, and supported.

My favorite quote about the importance of building an employee-focused culture comes from the legendary Southwest Airlines CEO Herb Kelleher, who said:

"If the employees come first, then (customers) are happy... A motivated employee treats the customer well. The customer is happy so they keep coming back, which pleases the shareholders. It's not one of the enduring green mysteries of all time, it is just the way it works."

Your culture must be about taking care of people, both inside and outside the organization, and the first group of people to take care of is the employees.

PRINCIPLE #3:
EMPOWER PEOPLE

We hire people for talent. It stands to reason that, once they are on the job, we ought to support them and let their talent shine through.

Letting their talent shine through takes two forms. First, we need to *give people the authority, the resources, and the organizational support they need* to solve problems in real time, during actual interactions with customers. As part of our organizational culture, we have to make sure that the team members who are interacting with customers are trained to *solve problems in real time* whenever possible and that they are praised for doing so. This means clearly celebrating the value of looking for solutions first. Where it is appropriate to do so, we want to give team members a certain amount of personal discretion in resolving customer issues, so they can turn Moments of Misery into Moments of Magic without falling into the trap of reciting the rulebook (something customers hate). For instance, we might tell people working on the front lines that they can take their own approach to resolving customer issues and making them feel good about working with us, up to a predetermined dollar limit. We make sure that they know they will never be criticized for acting on their own initiative as long as they act within the agreed-upon guidelines. If someone tries something different and makes a mistake, it will be treated as a learning opportunity for everyone. If someone creates a great new way of managing a customer issue, that will also be shared with everyone.

The second way we can empower people with talent is to *notice what their strengths are and play to those strengths.* In other words, find out what people are best at and love doing and then encourage them to grow and leverage that strength on behalf of the company, perhaps in an entirely new role. This approach to leadership may take a little time for you to implement, if it's not what you're used to doing right now, but it's worth practicing. At the end of the day, internal amazement means growing the team. It means helping each employee to develop and grow and make the most of their abilities. This requires having a certain amount of faith in your team's ability to grow and learn and contribute more over time. The issue here is how to make the best possible use of *human* resources. One of my favorite quotes on this topic comes from Steve Jobs, who said, "It's not the tools you have faith in. Tools are just tools. They work or they don't work. It's the people you have faith in or not."

PRINCIPLE #4:
PUT IT IN WRITING

The leader of the organization must come up with a brief, compelling statement outlining the purpose or mission of the company.

Ideally, this will be short enough for everyone to remember and understand, timeless enough to reinforce forever, and powerful enough to influence decisions and actions throughout the company. I don't much care what you call this piece of writing: purpose statement, mission statement, whatever. Just make sure it's compelling! My favorite example of this, and I've mentioned this at some level in my other books, is the guiding statement from the Ritz-Carlton Hotel. Founder Horst Schulze describes the process by which he came up with the hotel's now-famous credo:

"I understood what it means being a busboy and dishwasher, a waiter, a cook. I understood that. I've looked at it from their side, made a few beds. So I said, 'Okay I want to create an environment where the employees are really part of the organization.' And years ago when I was in doing my first job, I was 16 years old, I wrote an essay for... mind you, once a week we went to hotel school at the time... I wrote an essay and I named it, 'We are ladies and gentlemen,' meaning the employees in the hotel, 'And we serve ladies and gentlemen.' That's what I wrote as an essay and explained in there, 'We are ladies and gentlemen. If we are doing an excellent job, a first-class job, we are respected by the employee and we define ourselves by being excellent as ladies and gentlemen.' And with that motto, I started Ritz-Carlton and I said right from the beginning, you're not servants. Day one I said, 'We are not servants. *We are ladies and gentlemen serving ladies and gentlemen.*'"[1]

If you are not the company's leader, and there is no such statement and no sign of one emerging in the future, take the initiative and write such a statement for the team you lead.

PRINCIPLE #5:
CULTURE STARTS AT THE TOP

As you read through this principle, if you're not in a leadership or management role, you may be thinking, *This isn't for me.* This principle is for *everyone*, regardless of their role. Everyone must understand the leader's role and responsibilities related to the organization's culture in order to better understand both the culture and their role in supporting it.

Let's say your organization has publicly identified the value of *courtesy* as being essential to the company's mission. Let's say that your CEO has ordered that posters extolling the importance of *courtesy* be placed in every break room and every common area and that the CEO constantly mentions the importance of courtesy in company meetings. And let's say that this executive happens to be one of those who creates fear in the team every time they step out of the office. There's a disconnect. An executive can't yell at employees and then expect them to treat customers (and fellow employees) with courtesy. That company culture has not been built around the value of courtesy.

What's happening on the inside of an organization is always felt on the outside, by the customer.

Culture starts at the top. If leadership doesn't live the culture, the rest of the company won't either. If you are leading an organization, or a team, remember that everyone is looking to *you* to set the example. What is culture if it's not demonstrated and lived at the top? What is culture if it's not bought into at all levels of the organization? Culture is only meaningful, and only has an impact on customer loyalty, when it is lived as a team.

PRINCIPLE #6:
HIRE AND ASSIGN FOR AMAZEMENT

I'm not a hiring expert, but I can tell you this much: Some people are going to love doing a job where they get to listen to people for hours on end, understand their situation, empathize with them, and help them solve their problems. Other people are going to feel exhausted by that kind of job. But you know what? They may not realize that when they show up for their job interview. Make sure you know which applicant is which.

> When it comes to customer-facing positions, make sure you are putting the right person in the right proverbial seat on the bus.

There is an important exercise I occasionally do in workshops that is relevant to this discussion. I put a large whiteboard or flipchart in front of the audience. I ask the audience to shout out the traits of someone who would be good at customer service. As you can imagine, I get lots of answers. A few of them are:

Friendly, outgoing, funny, engaging, poised, empathetic, sympathetic, helpful, knowledgeable, good communicator, happy, confident, kind, responsive, positive, passionate, nice, honest, polite – and the list goes on and on.

What's interesting is that most of the traits you just read are *attitudes* – just a few are skills. A "good communicator" is obviously in possession of certain skills. You can argue that "knowledgeable" is also connected to someone's skill. But the rest are all expressions of the person's *habitual* attitudes.

My point is that you want to find a way to identify those attitudes. I'm not suggesting that the skills aren't important. They absolutely are. If a medical center needs to hire a skilled nurse, they are going to look at more than just an attitude. Nurses have to go to school, pass exams, get a degree and be licensed, and so on. Without that, all the people-first attitude in the world won't land someone a job as a nurse.

But when we hire new people, we do need to remember that, regardless of how strong someone's skills are, without the right personality, even a single employee we put in the wrong role has the potential to bring down a customer-focused culture. That person can make it very difficult for us to set up a process that consistently delivers Moments of Magic. We need to get a very clear sense of the applicant's personality *before* we make a job offer on a customer-facing position. And before we hire for any position, we want to make sure that the person's habitual attitude and personality match the culture we want to build and support.

PRINCIPLE #7:
MAKE SURE THERE IS A GOOD COACH

I look at the best teams in business – whether they are customer service teams, sales teams, accounting teams, operations teams, or leadership teams – and I ask myself, what makes them highly effective? The answer is always *team cohesion*. This is an outcome the team's leader is responsible for delivering. Nobody else.

> # The leader of a truly effective team is like the coach of a pro sports team.

That coach fulfills three essential responsibilities:

- Finding the right players to fill the right roles.
- Adjusting assignments and roles over time to adapt to new situations and play to people's strengths.
- Choosing players who will have the ability to work together well, ensuring that there is the right chemistry on and off the field.

This coaching role is a vitally important element of the "I'll Be Back" culture. We may have a bunch of rock stars on paper, but if the right people are not in the right roles pursuing the right goals, and there is no ability to work together, the results are not going to show up on the scoreboard.

In the next chapter, we'll look closely at customer service itself – and find out what parts of it are timeless and unchanging, regardless of technological and social changes.

KEY POINTS

- One interaction with one person is enough to create a long-lasting positive (or negative) impression of your company. As far as that customer is concerned, that impression is the reality.

- Customer service is not a department, but a philosophy to be embraced by everyone in an organization. It's part of the culture of a company.

- What's happening on the inside of an organization is always felt on the outside, by the customer.

- When it comes to customer-facing positions, make sure you put the right person in the right proverbial seat on the bus.

- The leader of the truly effective team acts as a coach, fulfilling these essential responsibilities:

  ▸ Finding the right players for the right roles.

  ▸ Adjusting assignments and roles over time.

  ▸ Ensuring that there is the right chemistry among team members.

CONVERSATION STARTERS

- Which of the seven principles discussed in this chapter is your team already doing a good job of following?

- Which of the seven principles highlights an area where there is the most room for improvement?

- What is an example of a time when an internal problem on your team led to a Moment of Misery for a customer? How could that internal problem have been handled better?

TAKE ACTION!

Share and discuss the seven principles discussed in this chapter with everyone on your team, and identify which ONE principle your team should be focusing on improving over the next week.

NOTE

1. Source: "Ritz-Carlton Founder Horst Schulze On Creating A Gold Standard" https://chiefexecutive.net/ritz-carlton-founder-horst-schulze-gold-standard/2.

CHAPTER 5

NOTHING HAS CHANGED IN CUSTOMER SERVICE

In November of 1989, Microsoft co-founder Bill Gates, already a billionaire at age 33, made a remarkable suggestion as he toured the Microsoft product support department's new building.[1] (Today, we would refer to the facility he was inspecting as a call center.)

Gates asked the manager in charge of one of the teams, "Mind if I take a call?" When was the last time you heard about a billionaire volunteering to help out at a call center?

The manager, of course, had no problem with letting Microsoft's #1 executive handle an incoming customer call. So, Bill Gates put on a headset, sat down at a cubicle, and took the next call in the queue. Here's how he answered the phone: "Hello, this is Microsoft Product Support, William speaking. How can I help you?"

Without further identifying himself, Gates chatted amiably with the customer, asked him why he had called, got clear on the details of the man's problem, and figured out what the challenge was. Once he knew that, he searched the product support Knowledge Base as any other employee would have done, evaluated the search results, spotted the best solution to the issue, and patiently talked the customer through the steps necessary to resolve the problem. The customer was thrilled with the outcome. Gates wrapped up the call and closed by saying, "And thank you for using Microsoft products."

Later, when the same customer called back with a follow-up question, he made a point of asking for "the nice man named William who straightened it all out."

HAS CUSTOMER SERVICE CHANGED?

Has customer service changed in the years since Bill Gates strolled through that call center, strapped on a headset, and took that call?

Many of the people I talk to answer, "Yes." They say things like, "Think how much has changed since 1989. The Internet was still in its infancy. There was no World Wide Web. The phrase 'social media' didn't even exist. No one had even heard of online reviews in 1989. Chat and chatbots were not part of our vocabulary. And AI, as in artificial intelligence, was something out of a science fiction movie. Of course customer service has changed!"

To which I have to say, I respectfully disagree.

The essence of customer service today is exactly the same as it was when Gates took that incoming call. And the way we want to approach it – Gates' way of approaching it – is exactly the same, too.

> # A customer comes to us with a problem, question, or need. They want their problem resolved, or their question answered, or their need fulfilled.

All of that is timeless. It is the essence of customer service. Ideally, we solve the problem, answer the question, or fulfill the need in such a way that customers think to themselves, *That was a good experience – I wouldn't mind going back there again.*

This basic dynamic is never going to change. Customers have expectations. If we do what Bill Gates did that day – if we listen to them carefully, get a clear sense of what they're looking for, and make sure their problems are resolved, their questions answered, and their needs fulfilled – they'll have the kind of experience that makes them feel good about coming back. They'll want to come back (even if we can't promise that the CEO of the company will answer their call the next time around).

Here's the beginning of the customer service process: The customer has a question they want answered or a problem or complaint they want resolved.

Here's the ideal end of the customer service process: The customer is happy.

It's that simple. Everything else is in the middle.

Yes. Much has changed socially, technologically and historically since 1989, and much more will change. A lot of things in the middle may shift around. A lot of technology may enter into the process. We may even design a process that makes customers feel happy without them having any contact with a human being at all! That's great if we can do it – and if that's what our customers want. But what we need to bear in mind is that the beginning and desired end result are never going to change.

We can't let ourselves get distracted. We can't let the technology people now have access to, the social changes we've all had to process, or anything else persuade us to take our eyes off the ball. We have to focus on the beginning and on the end. We have to figure out what kind of experience will generate the outcome that inspires the customer to think, *I'd like to do business with them again.* And to do that, we have to be willing to do what Bill Gates did – gain an understanding of what brought the customer to us in the first place.

The customer had a problem they thought we could solve, a question they thought we could answer, or a need they thought we could fulfill. If we don't know what that is, if we don't *listen,* we can't expect the customer to come back.

Often, when we get distracted, we end up giving the customer the experience we *think* the customer wants as opposed to the one the customer actually wants. We create a disconnect or a gap. How do we do that? By flunking what we might call the Bill Gates Test. We don't do what Gates did. We don't find out what the customer's issue really is. And until we find that issue and address it, we can't expect to deliver an experience that makes the customer think, *You know what? I liked that. I ought to go back there.*

SYNCHRONIZING THE CHANNELS

Something that has changed in the middle is that we may have more channels to synchronize than Bill Gates did back then. That doesn't alter the fact that we need to know what the customer's issue is. It just makes the task a little more intricate. When customers come to us with an issue, they may have made several attempts to resolve their problem before reaching out to us by phone. They may have filled out a form on their computer, searched our knowledge base online, tried to download our app, or sent us a message in a chat box (not realizing that the first couple of responses have come from an artificial intelligence program). This customer could well have faced multiple challenges in each of those environments. We need to find out what those challenges were. We have to make all those platforms work for the customer, and yes, that's a daunting task that requires careful thought and planning when it comes to resources, training, personnel assignments, and oversight. But the fundamental question remains the same: Are we going to find out what their issue is and leave them feeling fulfilled about the way we've handled that issue, or not? If the answer is yes, they are likely to come back and connect with us again. That is never going to change.

Suppose that customer gets frustrated with the challenges they experienced on one or more of our platforms. Suppose that customer is not happy with our response. Suppose that customer loses their cool. Suppose they start talking about how badly they've been treated, how confused they are, or how certain they are that they never want to do business with us again. What are we going to do?

Let me answer that question by posing another: What would you do if a close family member got upset and lost their cool with you? Would you walk away from the entire relationship? Would you say, "I'm sorry you feel that way, please go find another family to be a part of"? Of course not! Yet all too often, that's what we say to customers who get frustrated with our organization and lose their cool. We forget that they are communicating with us for a reason.

Even when they get upset – especially when they get upset – customers still want their problem resolved, their question answered, and their need fulfilled. We have to keep that in mind, especially when things get intense. We have to be ready, willing, and able to step back from the drama, de-escalate, and say something like, "I really want to find a way for you to stay with us. How can I do that?" And then work from there. That simple human appeal to maintaining and improving the relationship is essential. It gives us an opportunity to hit the pause button, reset, and do what the customer desperately wants us to do, even if they don't quite have the words to express what they want. They want us to *listen*.

Customers want us to listen, even when they don't come out and tell us that.

ONE MORE LESSON FROM BILL

Gates famously observed that "Your most unhappy customers are your greatest source of learning." The reality that someone is actively expressing unhappiness to us in the present moment may not feel great, but we need to remember that they're still choosing to communicate with us. They have not disengaged and moved on to a competitor. And that means that there is still a chance for us to turn a Moment of Misery into a Moment of Magic.

> Although the way we go about serving the customer may have changed over the years, the beginning and end of the customer's journey with us remains exactly the same.

Congratulations! You've reached the end of Part One, "The Basics of Customer Loyalty." In the next part of the book, we'll take a more tactical approach, and I'll share some powerful tools and ideas you can use right away to drive loyalty in your customer base.

KEY POINTS

- Customer service is simple. A customer comes to us with a problem, question, or need. They want their problem resolved, or their question answered, or their need fulfilled. This is timeless.

- Ideally, we solve the problem, answer the question, or fulfill the need in such a way that customers want to come back.

- Customers want us to listen, even at moments when they don't come out and tell us that is what they want.

- Unhappy customers can be our greatest source of information.

- Although the tools we use to serve the customer may have changed over the years, the beginning and end of the customer's journey with us remains the same.

CONVERSATION STARTERS

When was the last time you talked directly to a customer? How and when did that happen? (Note that the conversation could have been during a service discussion, a sales discussion, or even a random contact with the customer that didn't fall into either of those categories.)

What was the specific problem, question, or need that customer expressed to you, directly or indirectly, during that conversation?

Did the customer go away with their problem, question, or need addressed? Why or why not?

If you weren't able to give the customer exactly what they wanted, what were you able to do?

Are there procedures or guidelines in place for determining what people on your team can and can't do on their own to solve a customer's problem or issue? If there are, how could that process be improved? If there aren't, what should that process look like?

TAKE ACTION!

The next time you talk directly to a customer, be sure you do the following three things once the conversation is over:

1. Jot down a few words about *what that customer wanted.* Keep it simple.

2. Jot down a few words about *how successful you were in getting the customer where they wanted to go, or at least pointed in the right direction.* Again, keep it simple.

3. Share your results with others on your team. Encourage them to complete the same exercise.

NOTE

1. "The Top Four Soft Skills Any Employee Will Need To Become A Superstar," https://www.forbes.com/sites/theyec/2017/08/25/the-top-four-soft-skills-any-employee-will-need-to-become-a-superstar/?sh=468299d57d51 and "That Time Bill Gates Answered a Tech Support Call... and Crushed It," https://www.entrepreneur.com/article/289857.

PART 2

MAKING LOYALTY A REALITY

In this part of the book, you will get practical ideas and strategies for moving from repeat business to true customer loyalty.

CHAPTER 6

WANT TO BE AMAZING? JUST BE BETTER THAN AVERAGE... ALL THE TIME!

Here's a dream service scenario.

A well-dressed, smiling couple goes out to their favorite restaurant to celebrate a special night together. They order a nice bottle of wine. They have a great meal. Near the end of that meal, something remarkable happens. Their server wheels out a special dessert cart – even though the couple has not yet ordered dessert. When the couple sees what is on top of the cart, they gasp and laugh and kiss each other.

They see two small cakes, each topped by a single lit candle. When he reaches the table, the server says, "Congratulations! We hope you're having a wonderful tenth anniversary celebration tonight!"

The whole restaurant erupts in applause.

Maybe you're wondering: How in the world did the server know that it was their tenth anniversary? Here's the answer: He got lucky. He happened to overhear the husband wishing his wife a happy anniversary and saying that ten years with her felt like ten days. What happened after that had nothing to do with luck, of course. Once the server stumbled on that critical piece of information, he thought about how best to make the most of what he knew. He talked to his manager. He tracked down just the right desserts. He got two candles. And he created a customer experience that would never, ever be forgotten. That was a WOW customer service experience if ever there was one.

Bravo! Will that couple be back? Yes. Will they tell everyone in their circle about what happened to them? Yes again.

But here's the thing. When they come back next time, it won't be their tenth wedding anniversary, and they won't have an experience that compares to the one they had on their anniversary night. That experience was a triumph of execution, yes, but it was not something you could plan for ahead of time. And it's not a level of experience you can expect to repeat.

Why is this story important? Because people often think companies have to deliver a WOW customer service experience – on the same level those customers experienced on the night of their anniversary – over and over and over again. Guess what? That's impossible. More to the point, it's not what I mean by "amazing."

Amazement is *not* a matter of delivering over-the-top, WOW experiences every single time. Of course, it's great when you can deliver those, and if you find yourself looking at the opportunity to do so, you should do what that server did and take full advantage of the opportunity. But just as a good baseball team doesn't build a winning season around the "strategy" of turning triple plays every inning, you shouldn't try to execute a "strategy" of delivering nothing but WOW moments.

What you must do is *be better than average all the time.*

To be amazing, you cannot slip into mediocrity. It's that simple. Inevitably, of course, there are going to be problems. Customers are going to get less than your best. Mistakes are going to happen. That's just reality. Remember, though, that we're talking about the *overall experience*, not an isolated incident.

The overall experience is what matters. Our goal is to get the customer to use the word "always" – and to follow it up with something positive, as in: "I love doing business with them. They're always so helpful."

That doesn't mean there's never a problem. It means that when there is a problem, we *always* find a way to help, and we make sure that the problem gets fixed. The best companies have a system in place when there are problems and complaints, and they have properly trained their team to manage them. If there's a problem and it's not fixed, your customer is going to rate you at a one or a two. But guess what? If there's a problem and it's fixed properly, the customer will give you a five-star rating. Remember, *every Moment of Misery has the potential to turn into a Moment of Magic.*

When the customer's day-in, day-out experience is transformed by this way of looking at what's happening in their world, their ongoing relationship with your company changes. A problem comes up, and you're able to fix it and also do a little something extra – not because you want to put a Band-Aid on the problem or because you want to give all kinds of free stuff away, but simply because you know that this is the right thing to do in that situation.

You're doing the right thing and the customer knows you're doing the right thing. You make the *relationship* the priority, not the transaction. And the customer thinks, *Even when there's a problem, I can always count on them.*

Here's the truly remarkable thing: If we commit to being at least *10 percent better than average*, consistently and predictably, customers *will* rate us five out of five – and they will come back for more.

Delivering amazing service means delivering, consistently and predictably, an experience that is a little better than average – just 10 percent above average.

This means finding creative ways to turn the (inevitable) Moments of Misery that customers experience into Moments of Magic.

THE 10 PERCENT FACTOR

You may wonder how I came across this 10 percent formula. Some time ago, I had the chance to meet and interview Horst Schulze, who I've already mentioned is the co-founder of the Ritz-Carlton Hotel Group. It was a true honor, because I've been following his work for decades. Schulze told me that his goal was always to become one of the most recognized brands in the world, known for incredible service. I asked him how he went about doing this, and his response was both surprising and validating. Horst said that the key was to be consistently and predictably above average.

When I asked him how much above average one had to be to earn a reputation for incredible service, Schulze told me, without a second's hesitation, "Ten percent." Being just 10 percent above average all the time delivers amazement.

Schulze knew that if you delivered that 10-percent-above-average level of service *consistently and predictably,* without ever drifting back into mediocrity, customers will bump you up to a score of five out of five. And you will have earned it. Remember, a problem or complaint that is unresolved will get a bad score and a bad review online. The issues that are resolved properly will generate fives (on a scale of one to five) based on how well the issue was handled. It's often the attitudes – apathy, low empathy, impatience, etc. – that get companies a lower score. Of course, if the problem isn't properly resolved, it will result in a lower score, too. But this isn't as much about the problems/complaints that pop up. This is about the overall experience.

The moment your overall experience drops into mediocrity, you have problems.

And do you know what is most likely to make the experience inconsistent? A simple lack of empathy. My company surveyed over 1,000 people about what drives a poor customer experience. The top responses were: rudeness, apathy, and not being treated as a valued customer.[1] These are all symptoms of a lack of empathy with our customers.

The inconsistency that results from failing to empathize with our customers is the real enemy here. An inconsistent, back-and-forth pattern, where we sometimes deliver a good or above-average experience, but at other times, we just don't care enough to try to move above mediocrity, is what keeps us from being better than average all the time. That pattern may get us an overall rating of a three or a four, but it's not going to get us a five. Only the consistent, predictable delivery of an *above-average* experience gets us a five out of five rating. That's what inspires people to say things like:

"I like doing business there. The people are *always* so eager to make sure you get what you need."

Or:

"I'm going back to that site next time I need (whatever). They *always* get right back to me when I have a question."

Or:

"I should go there again. They're *always* so nice."

Put the 10 percent factor to work for your organization. How do you do that? By always being at least a little bit better than average and by finding ways to turn even Moments of Misery into Moments of Magic.

WHAT'S YOUR PROCESS?

Let's talk about how to turn around a Moment of Misery.

The first thing we should address is the fact that there needs to be a debriefing process for dealing with the problems that come up during our interactions with customers. Problems with customers are a fact of life. They're going to happen. The first time a given problem comes up, it's okay for us to deal with it by instinct. In fact, that's pretty much our only option, because we've never dealt with the problem before. But the second time the same problem comes up, we must follow a plan. That plan needs to be the result of our internal discussions about the challenge we faced the first time. We need to ask:

- What happened?
- Why did it happen?
- What's the best way to resolve it if it happens again?
- Can we keep it from happening again? If so, how?

With regard to that last item, we need to ask a parallel series of questions about *great* customer interactions (like the one I mentioned at the top of this chapter). Why? Because we want our people to be able to reproduce those kinds of experiences. When those WOW moments happen, we need to ask: What happened? Why did it happen? What's the perfect setting for this to happen again? How can we make it happen more often?

Your Moment of Misery debriefing should point you toward a *process*. Once you identify what happened and why it happened, you need to design an effective process for turning minor mishaps into major wins. It's vitally important to have a system in place when problems happen.

Let me give you an example of what I mean. I love a good hockey game. My favorite team is the St. Louis Blues. Not long ago, I went to a game where a puck skittered over the protective glass and hit a fan squarely in the head. This person was just a few rows in front of me. Within seconds, an usher was by the fan's side. Other than the cut on his head, he seemed shaken, but okay. What happened next was a *process* – a system that had been honed to perfection. The usher looked up at the JumboTron scoreboard, where there are numerous security cameras, and she crossed her arms above her head, giving the signal that there was an emergency in her section. In under a minute, a crew of medics and security people were beside the fan, helping to get the situation under control. They led the fan out to an ambulance. Later, they gave the fan an autographed hockey puck, an autographed hockey stick, and tickets to a future game. As they closed the door to the ambulance, the fan said, "This is the best hockey game I've ever been to!"

Talk about having a *system* in place for turning a (predictable) Moment of Misery into a Moment of Magic. If you're wondering how you and your organization can possibly deliver an experience that is consistently above average, you now have the answer:

Create a system for dealing with, and transforming, predictable Moments of Misery.

In the next chapter, I'll share the shortest customer service speech in history, the moral of which has a lot to do with turning around Moments of Misery.

KEY POINTS

- Delivering amazing service means delivering, consistently and predictably, an experience that is at least a little better than average.

- Lack of empathy is what usually keeps the customer from consistently receiving an above-average experience.

- WOW moments are nice, but it's more important to commit to delivering a customer experience that is consistently at least 10 percent better than average.

- Debrief on Moments of Misery. Find out what happened and why it happened.

- Create a system for dealing with predictable Moments of Misery and transforming them into Moments of Magic!

CONVERSATION STARTERS

- What is a common Moment of Misery in your world?

- What does a mediocre customer experience look and feel like in your world?

- What does a customer experience that is just 10 percent better than average look like in your world?

TAKE ACTION!

Identify a part of the customer experience in your organization that is currently average and come up with a plan to make it at least 10 percent better. Share the plan with your team.

NOTE

1. Source: 2020 Achieving Customer Amazement Survey. https://hyken.com/2020aca.

CHAPTER 7

THE SHORTEST CUSTOMER SERVICE SPEECH IN HISTORY

If you gave me thirty seconds to deliver a great speech about customer service, I could pull it off and still have about twenty-eight seconds to spare.

Sometimes, I take part in events where there are multiple speakers on the agenda, and I am chosen as the closing speaker for the event. This is a highly sought-after position, of course, and receiving it is a great honor... but being the last person on the agenda does carry with it certain occupational hazards. Sometimes, the speakers who are on the agenda ahead of you go on for longer than they should.

This happens more often than one might think, and it puts time pressure on everyone. When it happens, the person in charge of the event will approach me with a worried expression and say something like, "Shep, so-and-so ran long. Do you think you can cut five minutes from your presentation?" Usually this is not a problem.

Every once in a while, I'll be asked to cut even more off the running time. I'll never forget the time a client said to me, "Shep, multiple people have gone on too long. We've run out of time. You've only got two minutes. What can you do?"

I thought, *I can't even warm up lasagna in a microwave oven in two minutes. How in the world am I going to warm up this audience?* But I agreed to do what was necessary. The client thanked me profusely, leaving me to work out what would happen when I stepped onstage. I didn't know what I was going to do, but as the old saying goes, "The show must go on!"

But now, I had just two minutes to work with, instead of the forty I'd planned for. How in the world was I going to compress my message into that absurdly small amount of time?

As I stood backstage, I asked myself, "What is the simplest, easiest to remember, most common-sense strategy you can use in customer service?"

Then it hit me. I knew exactly what I needed to do.

The host began to introduce me. He didn't say anything about the fact that I'd lost thirty-eight of my forty minutes. He did say this, though: "Ladies and gentlemen, we've saved the best for last. It's my pleasure to introduce someone who is going to deliver some great, powerful insights on customer service. Give him a big hand, everyone. Shep Hyken!"

The crowd applauded. I walked out and greeted the audience. The applause died down.

I said: "Folks, we're almost out of time. So, I'm going to give you the shortest customer service speech in the world. Ready?"

A hush fell over the auditorium.

I looked at the audience. I smiled. I said two words:

"BE NICE."

Then I dropped the mike and walked offstage.

Okay, maybe it wasn't quite that abrupt, but it was pretty close. In reality, I went on to say:

"BE NICE. It sounds like common sense, doesn't it? But you know what? A whole lot of stuff that is supposed to be common sense really isn't all that common at all. BEING NICE heads the list."

While I was waiting backstage, I had realized that I'd written seven books on how to be nice. Being nice to customers consistently takes quite a bit of thought, planning, and practice. But as an overarching strategy, being nice is the best place to start. Supporting a BE NICE strategy means choosing from a vast array of tactics. Some of them, like smiling and greeting people authentically, are going to work no matter what business you're in and no matter what kind of customer you serve. Some of them are going to be unique to the business, the company, the situation, and the customer you target.

This is more challenging than it sounds. To be nice, we have to find out what "nice" looks like from the customer's point of view and then figure out what we have to do to deliver that experience consistently. When you do deliver it, you make it a whole lot easier for them to decide that they want to keep on doing business with you.

If you're serious about getting customers to decide to come back and do business with you again, be nice to them!

IN SEARCH OF NICE

So, here's the question we have to take on: What, specifically, does NICE look like in our customer's world? And how do we execute NICE?

This is a big question. We have to ask ourselves: What goes into a moment that our ideal customer will classify as us being NICE? What decisions and interactions support the NICE experience we want to deliver to that ideal customer? What clearly identified words, actions, and processes will create a sense of an emerging relationship, a desire to keep interacting with us and our organization, and a feeling of trust that is worth coming back for?

For instance, what, specifically, does it mean to be nice on the phone to a customer who calls us? What should always be said? What should never be said? What needs to be accomplished by the end of the call? How do we know it's been accomplished? How should the call end? What tools and training do we need access to in order to make that NICE experience happen?

What are the tools and processes we need to put BEING NICE into practical application – not just once, but time after time after time? Helping you to develop those tools and processes is one of the major goals of this book.

The search for NICE never really ends, but it does have to begin somewhere. So, let's get started on that journey right now by posing one of the most important questions in all of customer service, namely...

ARE WE NICE?

If we are the leaders of the team, we need to make a habit of asking ourselves a tough question: Are we delivering NICE? Would our customers say we are being NICE to them?

That question is worth considering closely. It forces us to examine our existing processes and team assignments.

Let me expand a little bit on the thoughts on hiring and culture I shared with you back in Chapter 4. Some time ago, I had the privilege of interviewing Jim Bush, the former executive vice-president of World Service at American Express. One of the takeaways he shared with me that I'll never forget connected directly to this concept of BEING NICE. Jim told me that if he was hiring a call center representative, and he had the choice between hiring someone with lots of call center experience who had the technological skills and knowledge of the software... and someone with none of that experience who had spent the last ten years working behind the front desk of a hotel, he would go for the latter every time. Why? Because he would know for certain that the former hotel employee is strongly people-oriented. They start the day with a head start on BEING NICE on a person-to-person level. That part of the job is not going to be a stretch for them. You can teach that former hotel employee how to use the software. But you may not be able to teach the call center veteran how to be nice on the phone for eight hours a day.

Consider another example. Let's say you're the owner of a restaurant and you hire a server. We'll call him Bob. Bob has never worked at a restaurant, but he has a background in customer service. As a matter of fact, Bob was a front-desk clerk at a very nice hotel. He understands how to deliver great customer service. He loves interacting with people. But he doesn't understand how to wait tables.

Behavioral style (which can also be categorized as "personality") is one side of customer service; the second side is the technical side. A technical customer service lesson might be to teach a restaurant employee from which side of the guest we should set down a plate and from which side we should collect the plate. No amount of past customer service background as a front-desk clerk will teach Bob that. And there are lots of other nuances that go into creating the perfect customer experience at a restaurant. We're going to need to teach Bob what those are.

The technical side of customer service is fairly easy to teach... but that doesn't mean the customer will have a great experience. The employee also has to be able to understand, and consistently respond to, the human side of customer service. It is the combination of these two that produces an experience that's greater than the sum of the parts. No matter how good the person is with the technical skill, they still need the personality to go with the technical skill in order to be perceived as BEING NICE by the customer.

My point is, BEING NICE takes both attitude and technical skill. The best people have both. The best companies recognize and make sure their employees have both.

If we're serious about making BEING NICE a constant and predictable outcome for the customer, we need to make sure we're teaching the right skills, yes – but we also have to make sure we have put the right people in customer-facing positions. This is a critical part of building customer loyalty, one that too many companies overlook.

In the next chapter, we'll take a closer look at how to build real customer loyalty.

KEY POINTS

- The central goal of customer service, and the starting point for getting people to want to come back and do business with us again, is very simple: BE NICE.

- BEING NICE is not necessarily easy. It usually takes quite a bit of thought and planning.

- The customer is the judge. We have to identify exactly what NICE looks like in our ideal customer's world. And we have to execute that.

- NICE has two sides: personality and technical skill.

- We want friendly employees who naturally enjoy interacting with customers and have the knowledge and skills necessary to answer questions and resolve problems.

CONVERSATION STARTERS

- What does NICE look like in your world?
- What are the most important technical skills that customer-facing staff in your organization must master?
- What happens when we have all the technical skills, but the personality of NICE is missing? How does that affect the customer experience?

TAKE ACTION!

Make a list of specific phrases, greetings, responses, and questions that create NICE in your organization's interactions with customers. For instance, how do you answer or conclude a phone call in a way that supports BEING NICE? What is the most common question you hear from customers, and how could you answer that in a way that supports BEING NICE?

CHAPTER 8

HOW TO CREATE REAL CUSTOMER LOYALTY

Phil is a barber. The story about Phil that I'm about to share with you is relevant to his world... and to yours. You could be running a barber shop, or selling microchips, or selling potato chips. It really doesn't matter. The principles Phil mastered to build loyalty in his customer base are the same principles you can use to build loyalty in your customer base.

Phil set up what he thought was a customer loyalty program. His program looked like a lot of these so-called loyalty programs: It was a little card he handed out to customers. Every time they came back to Phil's shop for a haircut, or brought a member of the family in, Phil or one of the people who worked for him would pick up a hole puncher and punch a hole in one of the little squares on the card that the customer presented to show that the customer had earned one "loyalty point." When a customer had accumulated ten holes in ten squares, meaning ten loyalty points, Phil gave them a free haircut.

Here's my question for you. Does that little card, all on its own, build loyalty to Phil's shop?

Of course not. By now, I hope it's clear to you that loyalty is much more than points and rewards. The vast majority of so-called "loyalty programs," while they may drive repeat business, are not loyalty programs at all. They are marketing programs. There's a big difference. Points or rewards programs can easily be copied by competitors. True customer loyalty, as we saw in Chapter 2, is driven by an emotional connection that the customer has with us. We must connect with a customer at a level that goes deeper than simply punching out a hole on a little card or creating a points system and asking them to take advantage of it.

To create real customer loyalty, we first need to understand the difference between loyalty programs and marketing programs.

Marketing programs can reward customers for behaviors we want (like repeat purchases) without creating any emotional engagement whatsoever.

Loyalty happens only when customers *have a strong, continuous emotional connection to the experience of working with you*, based on your delivering an above-average experience *all* of the time.

Here's what Phil's customer experience looks like right now:

- The customer schedules a haircut either by phoning in or going to Phil's website and using a drop-down menu to set a time. While some customers like the convenience of booking an appointment online, Phil likes his customers using the online option so he doesn't have to talk to them. That's the wrong reason! Phil didn't upgrade the technology because he was thinking about the customer; he did it because he was thinking about himself. Oops.

- Phil makes sure the shop is open at the appointed time, not one minute before and not one minute after. He says hello once the customer shows up for an appointment and shows the customer to the barber chair. Phil is a get-down-to-business kind of guy.

- Phil points to the wall with the photographs of the styles he offers and asks the customer which one he wants. He likes to stick to the menu. He doesn't respond well when customers have ideas of their own about what kind of haircut they want or when they come in with photographs of their own, showing a style they'd like him to reproduce.

- Phil gives the customer a haircut. That is what they're paying for. He's not much for conversation during this part of the process. Some customers are okay with that. Others would prefer a little conversation.

- When he's done, Phil shows the customer a mirror and asks, "What do you think?" This is one of the very few questions he asks during the entire customer experience. The two employees follow Phil's lead when they're giving haircuts; this is usually the only question they ask, too.

- Assuming the customer says it looks "Fine" (a word I'll have more to say about in a moment), Phil brushes the hair off them, leads them over to the register, and processes the payment. At this point, he also thanks them for their business and asks if they have a loyalty card. If they don't, he gives them one and punches out the first hole. Phil considers the act of thanking them for coming by to be the high point of the whole experience.

Does Phil have a process? He certainly does. Does he imagine that his process builds loyalty? Probably. But now comes the big question: What is Phil's process *missing*?

Back in Chapter 6, I shared with you the main obstacles to an above-average customer experience: *rudeness, apathy,* and *not being treated as a valued customer.*

What do those three elements have in common? A lack of *empathy and/or connection* with the customer.

That's what Phil's process doesn't yet have. He can hand out as many cards as he wants, and he can punch those cards with his hole-puncher every single time they reappear. He can *call* those little cards the centerpiece of his "loyalty program." But the reality is, what his process is delivering as an experience has zero empathy, and therefore it has zero emotional engagement with the customer. As a result, even though there is repeat business, it generates zero loyalty.

You get the picture. Phil's barber shop does not offer an amazing experience. It's not an above-average experience and it's not terrible. It's okay. But without the punch card – are people going to come back? I have my doubts.

Phil just doesn't offer enough of an emotional connection. And as soon as another barber shop opens nearby, that lack of an emotional connection will mean that there's an opening for the competition. The customer may well move on.

MOVING BEYOND "FINE"

Now, suppose Phil were to push back on this analysis. Suppose he were to say, "What are you talking about, zero loyalty? My process is great. And do you want to know how I *know* it's great? I'll tell you. My customers are *satisfied*. Every time I ask them what they think of their haircut, they give me the same answer: *It's fine!* That's satisfaction, isn't it?"

It's at this point that we would have to share an uncomfortable, but unavoidable truth with Phil:

Satisfaction is not loyalty. And "fine" is not where you want to be when it comes to your relationship with your customer.

This lesson applies not just to Phil. It applies to all of us. Our customers today have higher expectations than ever before. They're no longer comparing us to our direct competitors. What they're comparing us to is the last great experience they had – at a restaurant, say, or a hotel, or an online vendor like Amazon or Zappos. That's what we're all up against. The customer doesn't care what industry we're in or what product or service we offer. They're thinking, *Why can't they be as good as the last great service experience I had?*

Of course, it's important to satisfy your customers. No one can dispute that's essential. But you know what? There are some studies that tell us that 60–70 percent of satisfied customers don't come back! And here's why: *They're just satisfied.*

"Satisfactory" is right in the middle. It's average. It's mediocre. Satisfaction is a rating. Loyalty is an emotion.

How do you like your haircut?

It's fine.

I've got news for Phil (and everyone else): *Fine* is the F-bomb of customer service! Four letters. Starts with F. And you never, ever want to hear it from your customer.

Now, we'd be looking at an entirely different situation if Phil had asked that question of his customer, and the customer had taken a long look in the mirror, smiled, and said, "Mighty fine!" In fact just about *any* words before or after the word "fine" would have told us that Phil's customer had indeed had an above-average experience: "Darn fine!" or "Super fine!" or even "Fine and dandy!"

But Phil's customers didn't say any of those things. They said "Fine." And that means we're in F-bomb territory, which is dangerous. We're delivering a mediocre experience. We haven't yet nudged that experience up to the above-average, all-the-time, no-matter-what level that we need to be in if we want to create a *loyal* customer, as opposed to a *return* customer.

Let's say that you owned a restaurant, and you had this conversation with your customer:

"How's the food?" "Fine."

"How's the service?" "Fine."

"How's your experience?" "Fine."

How would you feel about that customer's experience? Hopefully, you would recognize there was a problem. You would need to ask a deeper question if you wanted to understand why the customer only felt "fine."

So, does fine really mean fine? NO!

Let's assume, from this point forward, that the word fine is really an acronym that stands for:

F: Faking a smile – Even though the customer is smiling an inauthentic smile, they aren't all that happy. The experience was just okay.

I: Insincere response – This is exactly what that fake smile is. It looks nice, but it's not real.

N: Never coming back – This is sometimes the result of an experience that's just fine or average, especially if there's an opportunity to have a better experience elsewhere.

E: Emotionless – The word "fine," with a smile, may look like a positive emotion, but remember, it's insincere. It's an automatic response. Customers don't have to feel anything strongly positive in order to send you that message.

This all comes together in a bold statement I found on the Internet one day. When I came across the following memorable phrase on images, posters, and t-shirts, I laughed out loud.

Fine is not fine! The scale goes *Great, Good, Okay, Not Okay, I Hate You, Fine!*

Here's the point: That punch card, or any similar marketing efforts, may give us a *return* customer, even when there's a consistently mediocre (read, "fine") experience. But we want more than that. We want a special *kind* of return customer, a *loyal* customer. Think of the loyal customer as being the center spot on a target, and the repeat customer is the ring encircling that center spot. We need to find a way to hit the bull's-eye and make a real emotional connection.

One of the single biggest factors in hitting that bull's-eye and creating true customer loyalty is *empathy* for what the customer is experiencing and dealing with in life. That's what makes the emotional connection possible. Customers who give you high marks on a survey may be telling you they're happy, but that doesn't mean they're loyal.

> ## Ratings don't indicate real emotional connection, which means they don't indicate loyalty.

Empathy starts on the inside, with employees. This brings us back to our conversation about culture, and it raises the question of how strong Phil's relationship is with the two people he employs as barbers. Never forget that what happens on the inside of an organization is felt on the outside by its customers. The way employees are treated has a *direct* impact on how the customers are treated. If our internal culture fosters empathy and emotional engagement, that will always have a positive impact on the customer's experience. So, the first thing Phil would want to do to deepen customer loyalty would be to make sure his two employees were happy. In addition, he would ask them about their ideas for improving the customer experience.

Phil could also increase the odds that his customers move into that loyalty bull's-eye by...

- *Engaging with conversation about what's going on in their world.* As consumers, we often choose the people we want to do business with based, not only on their technical skills, but also on their personality and their ability to connect with us as individuals.

- *Finding more ways to make people feel like socializing with each other while they're waiting for their turn in the chair.* Remember: Many customers see barber shops and hair salons as social centers. Phil's clientele is men. Lots of men like sports. Why not set up a TV and put a sports channel on and let the guys talk about the game?

- *Finding a way to stay in touch after the haircut.* This could be as simple as an online monthly newsletter or social media posts. These kinds of initiatives can be a lot of fun. Just make sure you have people's permission to send them email messages or communicate with them in public forums.

FOUR POWERFUL STRATEGIES FOR CREATING CUSTOMER LOYALTY

Here are some more ideas Phil could put into practice – indeed, that anyone could put into practice. Notice that each has a strong emotional component. Although you can identify the metrics that connect to repeat business, you can't always explain loyalty with facts and figures. There's inevitably an intangible emotional side to it. This is because loyalty comes from us understanding the customer's wants and needs, and then finding a way to act on that understanding to deliver an above-average experience. Here are four ways we can do that, no matter what industry we're in and no matter who our target customer is.

1. Reward Empathy

Reward and acknowledge employees who engage with customers on an emotional level and then follow through by supporting an ongoing relationship with the customer. The word "empowerment" is overused these days, but it's the best word I can find to describe what happens when we reward employees for connecting emotionally with customers and then doing something that delivers an above-average experience. We want to encourage our employees to come up with new ideas that put the relationship first. That means encouraging them, when it's appropriate, to break tradition and go outside the established policies and processes. The first step, of course, is that our employees must be properly trained. Once that piece of the puzzle is in place, the culture must allow them to take chances, and it must acknowledge and support them for doing so. If we're in a management position, we must lead the charge to advocate for this kind of empowerment, and we must never forget that ideas for delivering an above-average experience can come from anyone – from people on the front line to people who are working behind the scenes to the CEO.

2. Adopt a Hospitality Mindset

Our goal is to make the customer feel at home, whether the interaction is happening in person, online, or over the telephone.

You might think that's a stretch, or even impossible, within the context of your business, but I am here to tell you that it's just as realistic a goal to make the customer feel at home, metaphorically speaking, when they're getting a haircut, or buying a car, or visiting a website as it is when they are booking a stay at a favorite hotel. From a service point of view, we make customers feel "at home" when we make them feel welcomed, comfortable, and in the right place. So, we must never stop asking ourselves: Is the experience we are providing *welcoming*? Is it *familiar*? Is it *positive*? Does it set up a desire to *repeat* an interaction with our company? Asking these kinds of questions is what I mean by adopting a hospitality mindset.

3. Schedule a Regular "Loyalty Huddle"

This is essential to creating deeper levels of customer loyalty. Allot some time in your calendar to talk to the team about customer service and loyalty principles. These should be brief, regularly scheduled meetings – say, once a week for ten minutes – that keep the concepts of loyalty and emotional engagement front of mind. Consider these meetings opportunities for mini-training moments and reinforcement of the most essential loyalty principles. The behaviors that get repeated, reinforced consistently, and rewarded are the behaviors your people will put into practice.

4. Make It Personal

At the end of the day, creating loyalty can be much more than a business or organizational goal. It can be a personal goal, too, something that corresponds with how you behave and how you treat other people. In addition to improving customer loyalty, you also want to raise the level of loyalty and emotional connection in the most important relationships in your personal life. How? By making sure these people know they can count on you whether times are good or bad, and then following through on your commitments. Do that, and you will know that you have made creating and deepening loyalty a priority – not just at work, but everywhere.

If you are a leader, you will find that putting these four ideas into practice is a matter of personal honesty and authenticity. Your efforts will be perceived as genuine only if they are realistic expressions of who you are as a person.

In the next chapter, we'll look at how to make sure customers feel "at home" when they do business with you.

KEY POINTS

- To create real customer loyalty, we first need to understand the difference between loyalty programs and marketing programs.

- Marketing programs can reward customers for behaviors we want (like repeat purchases) without creating any emotional engagement whatsoever.

- Loyalty happens only when customers have a strong, continuous emotional connection to the experience of working with you.

- Satisfaction is not loyalty. And "fine" is not where you want to be when it comes to your relationship with your customer.

- Regular team "loyalty huddles" are essential for creating deeper levels of customer loyalty.

CONVERSATION STARTERS

- What is the difference between a loyal customer and a repeat customer?

- Who would you say are your most loyal customers – the top 10 percent? What influences their loyalty?

- How important is empathy as a value within your corporate culture? How important should it be?

TAKE ACTION!

Discuss, with your team, each of the four powerful strategies for creating customer loyalty, and create appropriate plans for implementation.

CHAPTER 9

WHERE EVERYBODY KNOWS YOUR NAME

Does the experience you deliver to your customers make them feel as if they are "coming home," as if they belong, as if they are "regulars," as if they are recognized and remembered and valued as individuals?

Finding a way to make that kind of experience happen consistently is a powerful way to deliver an above-average experience – a Moment of Magic. I call this approach the *Cheers* Factor. Now, I realize that I'm probably dating myself here, but I think some readers are old enough, or committed enough students of classic TV comedy, to recall the series *Cheers*. It first aired in 1982; it ran for over ten years and thanks to the Internet, people are still streaming the episodes in huge numbers. *Cheers* was set in a bar in Boston where a gathering of lovable eccentrics got together to socialize and relax and, yes, feel at home. In fact, you got the sense that the bar was *more* of a home to these characters than the places where they actually lived. The theme song gave the show its memorable tagline, "You want to go where everybody knows your name."

Here's the thing: We all want to go there.

Whenever we work with someone who truly makes us feel at home, someone who treats us like one of the regulars, someone who knows our name and knows what we like, guess what happens? *We want to go back!* This may be because we want to feel at home like that again... or it may be because we're curious about whether the experience will be as good the next time... or it may be a combination of the two. But one way or another, we are open to another conversation, another interaction, another chance to do business together. That is the *Cheers* Factor at work. And when it happens, it is truly magical. Let me give you a couple of examples from my own experience.

THE PANCAKE

I'll start with a simple one, an example that's easy for just about any business in just about any industry to replicate. A while back, I had breakfast at one of my favorite places, a restaurant called First Watch. On that particular day, I wasn't all that hungry, so I ordered just one pancake. Typically, when I add a pancake at this restaurant, they charge a dollar. When the server left the check on the table, I noticed they had charged me five dollars for the pancake. I asked the server, Tomas, about the seemingly high-priced pancake – and learned there was a difference between adding a pancake to a breakfast and ordering just a single pancake for breakfast.

Tomas was very nice about it, and I was happy to accept both the policy and the reasoning behind it. It made sense. No problem. Then he told me, jokingly, that the next time I came in, he was going to give me a pancake for a dollar! I thanked him and left him a very nice tip for his great service and his outstanding attitude.

Two weeks later, I went back to First Watch for breakfast. That day, we had a different server. I ordered my usual breakfast. A few minutes later, the server came back with a pancake. She said that it was compliments of Tomas, the gentleman who had taken care of us the last time we were in for breakfast. I looked over and Tomas gave me a wave and a smile.

I was impressed. Wouldn't you have been?

Up until that moment, I had two major reasons to like going to First Watch: They serve great food, and they have consistently friendly service. Nobody is perfect, but they have their system down and they seldom miss. Their servers are always welcoming and upbeat. I've been a customer of theirs since they opened their stores in St. Louis more than a dozen years ago. I always know what I'm going to get: good food and friendly, reliable service.

Now I have another reason. *They remember me.* Instant Moment of Magic!

Technically, of course, I realize that the entire restaurant didn't remember me. *Tomas* remembered me. But as we discussed in an earlier chapter, one employee *is* the company for the customer. For me, Tomas represented the restaurant and all the other employees. When he remembered me, it made me feel great about the whole restaurant.

When one employee remembers the customer, that means (from the customer's point of view) that the entire organization has remembered the customer.

Remembering your customers is huge. It's worth doing, worth training others to do, and worth rewarding whenever it happens. Why? Here are four good reasons.

1. *It makes your customers feel special.* Who doesn't like to be remembered and appreciated?

2. *It makes the experience personal.* I was remembered, but more importantly, I was given a special, highly personalized experience based on Tomas remembering our earlier conversation. I didn't even have to pay a buck for the pancake he gave me. How long am I going to remember that? Forever!

3. *It creates a connection with your customers.* People like being around people they feel they know. That's just basic human nature. We're each hardwired to want to spend time with people who remember us and pay attention to us. Recognizing and remembering someone is the first step toward making a special personal connection that sets you apart from the competition.

4. *Last but not least, it dramatically increases the likelihood of a return visit.* People like going to – and like going back to – places where they are remembered. It's simply part of good customer service. Just like the "regulars" in the classic sitcom *Cheers* kept showing up at Sam's bar, you want your "regulars" to keep showing up to do business with you.

How much effort does it take to remember a conversation with a customer? Not that much. How much goodwill do you create when you remember that conversation – and that customer – the next time he or she shows up? Massive amounts!

Simply remembering the customers you've talked to and re-engaging with what you talked about last time is a reliable recipe for a Moment of Magic. Use it! Help others to use that recipe! And reward them whenever they do!

Now, let's move on to a slightly more advanced example.

THE BUNNY IN THE MAGICIAN'S HAT

Personalizing the experience simply means making the customer feel the experience is unique to them. So, when Tomas sent over that pancake, with his compliments, that was personalization. It could have happened only to me, based on my previous interaction with him. And personalization can get much more focused and intricate than that. For instance, if I've stayed in a hotel previously, and made a special request, the hotel may note that request in my record, so the next time I stay at that hotel, they remember the request and ask me if I'd like the same thing again. I don't even have to ask.

But some hotels create far deeper personalization than that. A while back, I stayed at the Crowne Plaza in Lansing, Michigan. I've stayed at many Crowne Plazas in the past, and they are nice hotels. However, the experience at this one was unique. It was a highly personalized experience, an experience that truly made me feel like I was at home, like I was somewhere I belonged. The way the staff went about delivering that experience was remarkable, and it has since become a case study in personalization, one that I now mention regularly in my speeches and presentations.

Personalizing the experience simply means making the customer feel the experience is unique to them.

I travel around the world and log about 150,000 miles a year as a "road warrior." I also have hobbies. I do card tricks and magic. I also play guitar. So, now that you have all that background, here's the story I want to tell you.

I checked in at the Crowne Plaza. The person at the front desk was pleasant; once she knew who I was, she made a point of using my name. So, notice that this was already an above-average experience, because I've been made to feel at home. This is officially a Moment of Magic, and the *Cheers* Factor is definitely in play. They know my name. But what I want you to notice is that the personalization did not stop there.

When I walked into my room, I noticed a handwritten note attached to the little shoe-shine kit. It read: *This will work wonders on the shoes of a road warrior.*

I thought to myself, *Apparently they know I'm a frequent business traveler. Cool. But let's be honest – a lot of people who stay at this hotel are frequent business travelers. That could have been just a lucky guess.*

Then I noticed some chilled bottles of beer that had been set out for me. These were not just any bottles of beer, mind you, but two special brands called "Double Magician" and "Staff Magician." I'd never heard of these brands; apparently, they are local to Lansing.

I thought to myself, *That's no lucky guess. They know I'm a magician. Impressive.*

Next, I noticed a guitar. A handwritten note right next to it read, *We heard you were a musician. Thought you might enjoy making a little music during your stay! From your friends at the Crowne Plaza.*

I thought to myself: *WOW!*

Finally, when I returned to my room that night from delivering my program, I saw something unusual placed on my bed. Now, it's customary for a lot of upscale hotels to leave a wrapped mint or chocolate on the pillow or nightstand; this is a nice touch. But my friends at the Crowne Plaza had taken this idea to the next level. There on my pillow was a plastic top hat with a chocolate bunny in it – a visual representation of the classic magician's rabbit-in-the-hat trick!

I thought to myself: *Holy cow! Actually... holy chocolate bunny!*

I decided I had to find out who was responsible for this and say thanks for this unbelievable experience, which obviously required a certain amount of prep work before I even walked in the door. I did find out. That person is a young woman by the name of Robin Goodenough. Yes, that's her real name – and her effort and her commitment to customer amazement is much more than *good enough*! She and the Crowne Plaza team in Lansing went above and beyond the call of duty. What did they do? Simple. They Googled my name and found my profiles on Facebook, LinkedIn, and Instagram. It was easy enough for them to see what my interests were. From there, they wowed me with a truly personalized experience that I have been sharing with audiences and clients around the world.

Now: Am I saying that every business needs to do what the Crowne Plaza team did for every customer? No. But what I am saying is that there needs to be *some degree of personalization*. It's possible that in your business model, the level of personalization that Tomas delivered would be more appropriate. In the Crowne Plaza's world, this was the level of personalization that made sense. And it was spectacularly effective.

Some may find what the Crowne Plaza team did to be a little "spooky." I didn't. If anyone posts something on a social channel like Facebook or LinkedIn, they should anticipate that others will see it. And as for using the information I posted publicly for the

purposes of creating an amazing and personalized customer experience... well, there's absolutely nothing wrong with that. It made me
incredibly grateful to my friends at Crowne Plaza Lansing. They
created a truly memorable experience that made me think, *I can't
wait to come back and visit them again!*

And isn't that what it's all about?

BIG DATA, SMALL DATA, MICRO-DATA

In an era when we're all growing used to online retailers like
Amazon and Zappos welcoming us back to their sites, remembering exactly what we've ordered in the past, and making aston-
ishingly relevant recommendations about what we might want to
order next, a few important questions for customer service teams
come to the forefront:

Is that level of deep personalization what customers are likely to expect from us, both online and in person?

Answer: Sooner or later – yes. No matter what industry we are in,
no matter what platform we use, no matter how frequently or rarely
we interact with our customer, the bar has been raised in recent years.
Customer expectations are on the rise when it comes to personalization, and we are at a competitive disadvantage if we ignore that.

Does that mean we have to try to match these online giants step for step and investment for investment when it comes to making customers feel "at home" online?

Answer: No. For most organizations, that's not a realistic goal,
and fortunately, it's not always necessary in order for you to compete for, and win, the battle to turn one-time customers into repeat

customers and to turn repeat customers into loyal customers. Create your own experience, one that's distinctive to your company!

So, what approach should we take when it comes to personalizing our interactions with online and in-person customers?

Answer: Start with the information you have... and build the personalization experience from there. Specifically, start with what I call *micro-data*.

It's very easy to get distracted by tools and applications that require a big investment and a lot of analytical ability to make sense of the information. When it comes to using what we know to personalize the customer experience, wherever that experience may unfold, I believe in following the wise counsel of President Theodore Roosevelt, who said, *"Do what you can, with what you have, where you are."*

With that guidance in mind, consider that the information you have, right now, about your customers and your prospective customers can be broken down into three basic categories:

Big Data

Large amounts of data can be overwhelming, but they can also tell a story. Big Data can help you spot major shifts in the overall market you serve. Depending on your customer base and the analytical tools available to you, there is information you *could* uncover that will tell you what direction your customers are headed and what their preferences and choices are likely to look like six months, a year, two years, or even further down the line from now. Big Data is all about identifying trends involving more than one customer. (For instance: Are your customers, as a group, more likely or less likely to book hotel rooms in August than in January?) Although this kind of information is strategically important, I'm going to suggest that it's not *directly* relevant to the goal of inspiring an individual customer to come back and do business with you again.

Small Data

This is information about different *groups* of customers you serve. They're not all identical. There are segments, and customers within those segments act and behave differently from one another. For instance, some of the people who book rooms at the Crowne Plaza are business travelers, while others are couples out to share a romantic weekend together, and still others are families on vacation. These are very different groups with different motivations for showing up. This information is important to understand at a basic level if you want to inspire a customer to come back and do business with you again. You need to have a working knowledge of the various segments of the market that you serve.

Micro-Data

This is data that reveals what a *particular individual customer* is interested in, did or did not do, preferred, or purchased. This is vitally important information if your goal is to get the person to come back next time. We can make our analysis of Micro-Data as simple or as sophisticated as we want. It might take the form of Tomas at First Watch noticing a familiar customer and remembering a recent conversation with that customer – and then sharing that information with a fellow server at the restaurant. Or it might take the form of Robin Goodenough at the Crowne Plaza doing a quick Google search on an incoming guest and finding a way to dramatically enhance that guest's experience based on what she learned. *Notice that both of these examples don't require huge investments in software or technical training.* Of course, there are plenty of ways to leverage Micro-Data in more sophisticated ways, like updating your CRM system to include information on specific customer requests and purchases. The point is, securing, recording, and acting on Micro-Data is a *top* priority when it comes to personalizing the experience. It's what both Tomas and Robin did. And it's what you and your team should be doing, too.[1]

> # Do what you can, with the information you have or can easily locate, to personalize the interaction with a given customer.

If you do that, you will create the kind of experience that makes the customer think, *I should go back there!*

In the next chapter, we'll look at a strategy that can give you a powerful and enduring edge in the never-ending battle for customer loyalty.

KEY POINTS

- Personalizing the experience simply means making the customer feel the experience is unique to them.

- When we work with someone who personalizes the experience, we want to work with them again.

- When one employee remembers the customer, that means (from the customer's point of view) that the entire organization has remembered the customer.

- Big Data is data that reveals trends about your customers as a whole.

- Small Data is information about different groups of customers you serve.

- Micro-Data is data that reveals a particular individual customer's interests.

CONVERSATION STARTERS

- As a customer, when was the last time someone at a business remembered who you were and made you feel at home? What specific factors contributed to that feeling?

- What could your organization do to make that kind of experience happen more often for your customers?

- What part of the customer experience you currently offer would be easiest to personalize?

TAKE ACTION!

Greet a repeat customer by name and thank him or her for doing business with your company.

NOTE

1. Note that I am proposing that you use legally gathered Micro-Data to make the experience better for the customer right now or in the immediate future – not that you sell the customer's data to other parties for later use, without the customer's knowledge or permission.

CHAPTER 10

WHAT DO YOU STAND FOR?

What if you could gain a competitive edge in the battle for customer loyalty, an advantage that would instantly set you apart from the competition?

Well, you can. The path I'm talking about is not for everyone, but if you decide that it's the right path for you and your organization to walk down, you could be looking at the proverbial game changer, the kind of distinction that creates not only committed, long-term, repeat business, but active *advocacy* on behalf of your brand on an ongoing basis.

Curious about how you might be able to make that happen? Good. Let's continue. Have you ever stopped to ask yourself:

- What is our mission?
- Do our customers know what cause we stand for as a company and why we stand for it? (Side note – you may not stand for any cause at all, and it's okay if you don't. But if you do, there are some intriguing possibilities to consider.)

- Can our customers quickly understand what kind of difference we are aiming to make in the larger world, not just in some passing way but as an integral part of our business model?

These are powerful and important questions, and yes, I do recognize that not all businesses are built around a social commitment.

But if these questions *do* resonate for you and your organization... if you *can* align your business with something you believe in strongly and your customers are likely to believe in just as strongly... then you may be in a position to leverage one of the most powerful and enduring strategies for generating repeat business, loyalty, and customer advocacy: *conscious capitalism.*

The conscious capitalism idea is the brainchild of Whole Foods co-founder and co-CEO John Mackey and marketing professor Raj Sisodia, co-authors of the influential book *Conscious Capitalism: Liberating the Heroic Spirit of Business.* Conscious capitalism is, in essence, a new business philosophy. Like many philosophies, it has its adherents and its detractors. There is no moral requirement to either believe in a given business philosophy or to condemn it; what is most important is to understand it and decide for yourself whether it works for you and your organization.

Mackey and Sisodia's philosophy embraces free-market capitalism as the most powerful model for progress and cooperation in human societies, but it also acknowledges the human desire to aspire to and achieve more than financial wealth. Conscious capitalism does not demonize profit-seeking, but it does advocate on behalf of the idea of incorporating important common interests into a company's business plan.

Basically, what Mackey and Sisodia are saying is, "Yes – turn a profit, but do it in a way that serves the interests of all major stakeholders in a company."

Mackey and Sisodia define four guiding principles in support of their approach to business:

HIGHER PURPOSE

They maintain that a business that commits to the principles of conscious capitalism focuses on a clearly defined purpose, one that goes beyond simply turning profits. As the business pursues that purpose, it engages, inspires, and improves relationships with its critical stakeholders.

STAKEHOLDER ORIENTATION

Mackey and Sisodia hold that businesses have numerous stakeholders and that among these are customers, employees, major investors, shareholders, suppliers, and perhaps even people who are not directly connected to the business, but touched by it. While most companies focus exclusively on delivering a financial return to their shareholders as their sole priority; by contrast, a conscious business focuses on serving the entire "business ecosystem" to create and optimize value for all of its stakeholders.

CONSCIOUS LEADERSHIP

Leaders at conscious businesses, Mackey and Sisodia maintain, emphasize a "we" mindset over a "me" mindset in their efforts to move the business forward. As a result, they work to cultivate a more collaborative and farsighted approach when it comes to pursuing the enterprise's business objectives.

CONSCIOUS CULTURE

The organizational culture is the collection of principles and values that govern how the business makes decisions and undertakes actions. A conscious culture, according to Mackey and Sisodia, is one where the principles of conscious capitalism animate all aspects of the enterprise and create a sense of cooperation and trust, not just among the employees, but in interactions between employees and customers.

We could look at Mackey's company Whole Foods (now owned by Amazon) as an example of conscious capitalism. How has the company distinguished itself in a brutally competitive grocery market? Take a look at the company's stated core values:

- *Selling the highest quality natural and organic foods.*
- *Satisfying and delighting their customers.*
- *Promoting team member growth and happiness.*
- *Practicing win-win partnerships with suppliers.*
- *Creating profits and prosperity.*
- *Caring about the community and the environment.*

All of those values are powerful, but note how the first and last ones create and support a sense of shared purpose with a particularly critical group of stakeholders: consumers. Many shoppers feel that traditional grocery outlets don't offer enough natural and organic options. When it comes to making the highest-quality natural and organic foods available to those customers, Whole Foods is in a league of its own: At 500 North American locations, it sells products free from hydrogenated fats and artificial colors, flavors, and preservatives, and it is a USDA Certified Organic grocer in the United States. The company sells only products that meet its internal standards for being "natural," and it has a strong commitment to transparency and responsible food labeling. If that's something that's important to you as a consumer, you're going to notice when you pass a Whole Foods store in your neighborhood, and you're going to be more inclined to consider shopping there.

What about that final core value: *Caring about the community and the environment*? Suppose that's just as important to you as a shopper, or perhaps even more important to you, than getting the lowest possible price at checkout? How does that affect your decision about whom to do business with – and whom to keep doing business with? There are millions of consumers for whom community and environmental issues are vitally important, who shop at Whole Foods, at least in part, because they feel confident that doing so is helping to support communities they care about and respect the environment in which they live. When they learn that the company is a major purchaser of "green power" (that is, power from renewable energy sources), they are likely to decide that the money they spend at Whole Foods is doing something more than just filling up the cupboards. They may conclude that, by shopping at Whole Foods, they are part of something larger than themselves. And when they find out about the actions of the company's charitable initiative, Whole Planet Foundation, they may well feel more inspired, and more engaged, than they do when they shop at traditional competitors. Here is a brief summary of the Foundation's mission:

> *Whole Planet Foundation is a private, nonprofit orga-*
> *nization established by Whole Foods Market and*
> *dedicated to poverty alleviation. We aim to empower*
> *the world's poorest people with microcredit in places*
> *where Whole Foods Market sources products.... The*
> *foundation has authorized $101 million through*
> *microlending partners worldwide, funding 4.3 mil-*
> *lion microloans and over 22 million opportunities for*
> *microentrepreneurs and their family members.*

If that kind of commitment resonates emotionally and positively with you as a shopper, wouldn't that emotion make you more
likely to shop at Whole Foods—and keep shopping there? Doesn't
it make you more likely to share how you feel about Whole Foods
with friends, relatives, and acquaintances?

By the way, if you are curious about the bottom-line business
impact of conscious capitalism, consider this: In 2017, the last year
for which figures are available, Whole Foods reported over $16 bil-
lion in net sales – not an insignificant figure. (Amazon certainly
thought the company was doing something right. They purchased
it for $13.7 billion in cash!) In early 2019, an InMarket study ana-
lyzed over 50 million shopping trips and concluded that Whole
Foods was in the top tier in terms of producing repeat business
from its customers, ranking 16th out of the over 100 national and
regional chains with over 50 locations. That's significantly better
than the rest of the industry. Other chains have different strategies
for creating loyalty among shoppers, of course. I'm not saying that
those strategies are inherently better or worse than Whole Foods'
strategy, but I am saying that Whole Foods' strategy has delivered very strong results over a sustained period and, if conscious

capitalism is something you're considering for your business, it is worth examining closely.

Impossible to ignore in any conversation about Whole Foods is Amazon's headline-grabbing strategic decision in 2017 to purchase the company and the inevitable follow-up question: How much has the company changed since then? As of this writing, Amazon has made noticeable changes in terms of team workloads, discounting, and incentives offered to Amazon Prime members, and some of these changes have rankled long-time employees. But Amazon has made *no* noticeable effort to move away from the company's basic brand message, its commitments to customers, its core emphasis on premium-quality organic food offerings, or its charitable work on behalf of causes that support environmental activism and awareness.

Like a lot of big companies that become subsidiaries of even bigger companies, Whole Foods has experienced some internal shifts, and not all of those shifts have been popular with workers whose tenure extends to the period before the parent company stepped in. While it was probably inevitable that Amazon would look for ways to do things like give Prime members better pricing, Amazon's leadership appears to have respected the Whole Foods value proposition: Fresh, organic, transparently labeled food is important enough to pay a little extra for, and so is the habit of doing business with a company that is strongly committed to responsible environmental stewardship. And yes, people are still coming back, in large numbers, to do business with Whole Foods because of that value proposition.

WHAT DOES ALL THIS MEAN FOR YOU?

So, what does conscious capitalism mean for you and your company? It means that if you can make a convincing case for what you really stand for as an organization – and if you can back that case up with authenticity, action, and commitment – you may well be able to forge a powerful and long-lasting bond with a portion of your target market and get people excited about coming back to do business with you on a regular basis. Another name for this approach to business is *cause marketing.*

In a moment, I'll be sharing some other examples of successful cause marketing initiatives that have created awareness, engagement, and extraordinarily high levels of customer loyalty for the brands they represent. Some of them you will probably recognize; others, you may not have heard about. Consider them all. One or more of these true stories, or the Whole Foods story I just shared with you, may spark an idea about a cause marketing initiative that could be a good fit for your team and/or your organization. This is not just for leaders! If you see something that inspires you, share it with colleagues and management... and see what happens.

Let me preface what follows with an important disclaimer: If you decide to do this, you must be all in. An inauthentic cause marketing campaign, one that isn't connected to your company's core principles and whose commitments are not shared by stakeholders, is worse than no cause marketing campaign at all. Imitating someone else will not do the trick.

If you decide to pursue a cause marketing initiative, make sure it is one that the whole team buys into and that is authentic to who you are as an organization.

Let me repeat, because the point is worth emphasizing, that cause marketing is not for everyone. Some business models simply aren't suited to it. If you read the stories in this chapter and determine that this line of engagement with customers isn't right for you, that's actually a good outcome. Why? Because, as I shared earlier with you, not everything in this book is going to be right for every company. My goal is to give you plenty of options, spark your creativity, and get you and your team thinking about the strategies that *will* be a good fit for your market and your mission. (In Chapter 15, I'll help you pull together all the good ideas you've come across in these pages and give you a framework for brainstorming and planning with your team about the very best ways to make "I'll be back" a response you hear much more regularly from the customers in your world.)

With all that having been said, consider the following powerful examples of cause marketing initiatives in action, and ask yourself whether something similar could drive engagement and loyalty among customers in your world.

Salesforce

Salesforce provides the world's leading customer relationship management (CRM) service and sells a complementary suite of enterprise software applications. The company has an innovative integrated philanthropic approach that it calls the 1-1-1 model. Employees donate 1 percent of their paid time doing work they really care about for a charity of their choice. Salesforce gives 1 percent of its services to people and organizations in need. And the company gives 1 percent of its equity to a charity that can make a difference. As this book went to press, the company has given more than $240 million in grants, 3.5 million hours of community service, and product donations for more than 39,000 nonprofits and educational institutions. The firm encourages other companies to follow its lead and adopt the 1-1-1 model in their world. Here's a potent quote from Marc Benioff, Chairman & CEO of Salesforce: "The business of business is improving the state of the world." Powerful stuff!

Bombas

Offering a new twist on an extraordinarily popular and enduring concept, online clothing retailer Bombas matches each customer purchase with a parallel donation to a cause that matters deeply to those customers: aid to those who are experiencing homelessness. This initiative is not a superficial add-on to an existing business model. It is deeply embedded in the company's identity. The company's website reads: "We're Bombas. We believe a more comfortable world is a better world. Everyone, no matter their circumstances, deserves to put on clean clothes that feel good. So we perfected socks and t-shirts you'll want to live in. Created apparel you'll never want to take off. And for every item you purchase for yourself, we donate an item to someone affected by homelessness."

ONEHOPE

On its website, ONEHOPE says, "We make great wine for the good of others." Every bottle of ONEHOPE wine a customer buys makes an impact, because a portion of the purchase price supports charitable causes around the world. The company has built a school in Guatemala, funded clinical trials for breast cancer research, planted a forest in Indonesia, provided millions of meals for children in need, found a forever home for tens of thousands of pets, and delivered hundreds of thousands of vaccines to end tropical diseases. The ONEHOPE value proposition is unforgettable: "Together, we have proudly donated over $5 million by sharing wine and giving hope." That number will have gone up by the time you read these words. And yes, the wine itself gets good reviews.

USA Mortgage

USA Mortgage sponsors an employee-driven program that supports a diverse range of carefully chosen charities that are near and dear to employees' hearts. Over the years, the program has sent a new Xbox to fulfill a bucket list item for a terminally ill child, supported affordable housing via Habitat for Humanity, and given support to veterans. I include the company here because of its emphasis on engaging employees – who are also stakeholders – as an integral part of the cause marketing initiative. Of the program, the company writes, "We have a deep commitment to be personally involved with each story and to walk alongside these charities rather than in front of them. Our employees are known for going above and beyond the call of duty. USA Mortgage wants to be at the forefront and the most visible proponent of development and fundraising for charitable causes in our communities. We come together and stand together."

Keeley Companies

Keeley Companies provides services and solutions in the construction, infrastructure, technology, development, logistics, and wireless sectors. Employees are known as Keeley'ns, and many are active in the innovative #KeeleyCares program. Keeley'ns can add charitable logos to the company's Wall of Compassion by getting five other Keeley'ns actively involved, raising $1,000 within the year, and completing 40 hours of service within the year. The #KeeleyCares fund also matches funds raised for approved nonprofits and offers up to two days of paid time off for every 50 hours of approved volunteer time with a donation of $100. I list them here because an engaged workforce is an important prerequisite for consistently delivering a moment of amazement – and the employees at Keeley Companies are definitely engaged. The company's charitable outreach has the triple effect of defining the company powerfully and positively for consumers, making the world a better place, and raising morale levels through the roof. What more could you ask for?

A SIDE NOTE

Companies, of course, are not static entities. Monitor them over decades, and you will notice that some grow, while others don't. Some revise their business model. Some close up shop. Years ago, I remember reading the breakthrough book *In Search of Excellence,* by Tom Peters and Robert H. Waterman, Jr. The book, which is still a great read and an immensely influential collection of case studies, examined management best practices at successful organizations. A lot of the companies that were successful in 1982, when the book came out, were no longer around a decade later. That doesn't mean that all the best practices the book identified were irrelevant. What it means is that the management philosophies, the people making the decisions, and the larger economy changed over time. The same is true of the companies whose business models I have shared with you here and indeed all the companies I am sharing with you in this book. Their appearance on these pages is not a prediction of their market position, or even their existence a decade from now. They are here to give you ideas and insights you can put to work in your world.

There are many different ways to engage customers emotionally and, at the same time, make a contribution that matters to the world in which you live. Take a close look at how these companies have given something back and created powerful loyalty in their chosen customer base, and consider whether such an approach might make sense for your organization.

In the next chapter, we'll look at how giving your customer more and better self-service options can dramatically improve customer loyalty.

KEY POINTS

- Cause marketing, also known as conscious capitalism, is a powerful and enduring strategy for generating repeat business and loyalty.

- Make a convincing case for what you really stand for as an organization – and back up that case with authenticity, action, and commitment – and you may be able to forge a powerful emotional bond with customers.

- Aligning your business with something you and your customers strongly believe in can create dramatic improvements in customer loyalty.

- Cause marketing is not right for every company.

- If you do decide to pursue a cause marketing initiative, make sure it is one that the whole team buys into and that is authentic to who you are as an organization.

CONVERSATION STARTERS

- What is your mission?
- Does your customer know what cause you stand for as a company and why you stand for it? (Remember, you may not stand for any cause at all, and it's okay if you don't.)
- Is the cause you share with customers an integral part of your business model? (If the cause stopped being important to your company without changing your operations in any way, then it is not an integral part of your business model.)

TAKE ACTION!

Decide whether a cause marketing initiative is right for your business, and if so, what it might be.

CHAPTER 11

SELF-SERVICE: GIVE THE CUSTOMER CONTROL... IF IT CREATES A BETTER EXPERIENCE

Sometimes, people misunderstand me when I say that self-service is one of the keys to developing and sustaining customer loyalty.

Sometimes, they think I'm talking about an experience like being able to go to the gas station and pump your own gas, without the hassle of having to go in and wait in line to pay for it. Or they think I'm talking about being able to use self-checkout at the grocery store and avoid the longer line to the cashier. Or they think I'm talking about including a Frequently Asked Questions page on a website so customers can avoid having to call the customer support department.

While there's certainly nothing wrong with any of these options, we need to understand that, although they may have helped us create a better experience – a Moment of Magic – when they first came on the scene, they have since become *expected by customers.* If we want to deliver an experience that is above-average, we need to find a way to put customers comfortably in the driver's seat, in a way they *haven't yet* experienced and *don't yet* expect.

> # We need to be constantly on the lookout for *new* ways to let customers choose what happens next.

PUT THEM IN THE DRIVER'S SEAT

Giving control to customers in a new way and making them feel more comfortable and more in charge of where they're going and how they're getting there is a great way to build loyalty. We can find new ways to put the customer in control before the purchase, during the purchase, or after they have started working with us. We can make this happen as part of *any* interaction we have with a customer. It really doesn't matter where it shows up. Great self-service options can deepen any relationship we have with any customer.

Once you give customers a new, welcome sense of personal control along with tools they actually like to use, tools that work and get them where they want to go, you deepen their sense of confidence in working with you. You make it more likely that they will want to come back and do business with you again. And that, of course, is what it's all about.

Self-service is one of the most important and powerful new roads to amazement... and it's only gaining in importance with time. We must stop thinking of a robust, constantly improving self-service option as a "nice to have" offering and start thinking of it as what it has become: a core expectation of today's consumers. The vast majority of people, in my experience, expect some kind of self-service application from the people and companies they work with. If you doubt this, ask yourself when was the last time you visited a record store in person. (If the term "record store" is unfamiliar to you, we can consider this point made. Google it for a quick history lesson.)

We now live in a culture of downloads, digital tools, and remote, self-paced purchasing. Self-service is a growing part of that culture, and it's a trend that has only intensified since the onset of the economic and lifestyle shifts that were brought about by the emergence of the global pandemic. We no longer live in an era when a phone call or an in-person visit is necessary to complete a transaction or check on the status of an order. People want to complete some or all of the process themselves. It's estimated that 40 percent[1] of consumers now prefer self-service over human contact with the company they are buying from; 73 percent[2] of customers say they would rather go to a company's website than to social media, SMS text messaging, or live chat for support. In such an environment, offering the right self-service options needs to be considered "table stakes." It's what you put down on the table just to be able to play the game.

Consider, too, that most of today's consumers are comfortable doing quite a bit of online research before they make a purchase. Make it easy for them to find the information they need online. And make it easy for them to find out what your company's biggest fans have to say about you.

SELF-SERVICE DELIVERS AMAZEMENT

To understand why setting up and expanding your organization's self-service options is a must, not an option, consider an example that just about everyone can relate to: air travel. As you read through what follows, think about the reasoning behind what the airlines did and how passengers reacted to it.

Once upon a time, airline passengers were used to dialing a phone number and talking to a human being in order to book a flight or waiting in line at the airport itself. This approach often entailed long wait times – which passengers put up with because there was no alternative.

Now, passengers seldom call an airline to make a reservation.[3] Instead, they opt to use the self-service solution on a phone app or to visit the airline's website to book tickets. They can check in online and even download their boarding pass to their cell phone. The easier to use and the more intuitive these self-service tools are, the more in control the passenger feels – and the more likely they are to consider flying with that airline again. The more often, and more easily, the flier uses the airline's self-service options, the greater the competitive advantage for that airline. *Offering self-service options to the flying customer is now a core expectation!* It's what customers already want and feel they have coming. We may think of these tools as an extra, as an add-on, but that's not how the customer views it. The big question a lot of customers ask is, *whose* self-service tools are the *easiest* to use?

So, if we're working for an airline, and we want to maintain an advantage in the marketplace and build loyalty, we can't sit on our laurels. Our self-service process must be updated constantly and with an eye toward delivering new levels of intuitiveness, autonomy, and ease of use to prospective fliers.

Self-service is not a destination. It's a direction.

If you want to compete in this wireless world, you should be prepared to offer and constantly upgrade a seamless, easy-to-use digital system, ideally one that is actually fun to use, one that puts people in control of the entire process, without glitches or hiccups. The easier and more intuitive and time-saving the self-service process is, and the more often it is seamlessly updated, the more likely the customer is to keep on using it.

STRIKING THE BALANCE

Self-service systems must strike a careful balance: They must always put the customer in charge of what happens next, but never leave the customer feeling abandoned. In the case of airline booking systems, they must give passengers a welcome feeling of being in the driver's seat... while still being taken care of.

If the customer needs to, or wants to, they must be able to reach out to a human being. We must never imagine that the kind of continually evolving, continually improving self-service system we are talking about can be entirely self-contained. Part of our commitment to letting the customer be in full control of the experience is letting them choose when it's time to raise their hand and get our attention.

A good self-service option puts the customer in the driver's seat, *until and unless* they feel like asking for help with the driving.

At that point, a human must be ready to step in. (For a deeper dive into this important point, see Chapter 13, "You Can't Automate a Relationship.")

I believe every good self-service system must meet this standard if it's going to create repeat business and customer loyalty. The system must incorporate an option to connect easily with a human being if and when the customer chooses. There must always be an option *not* to use the self-service option! After all, a self-service solution doesn't mean you don't offer customer service. We are committing to implement and constantly improve these systems for one reason: to *enhance* the customer experience. That means giving people access to traditional one-on-one support when *they* decide that's what they want.

Of course, if we design and upgrade the systems properly, people will be strongly motivated to do the vast majority of the driving on their own and, most of the time, will opt to do just that. As a frequent flier, I have certainly had plenty of experience using apps on my phone to set up my own flight reservations. Once I got used to using the airline's phone app, I realized that there were all kinds of things I could look up easily and quickly – flight times, boarding times, flight status – that once upon a time would have entailed waiting on hold to talk to a person. If I could do that more quickly and easily just by touching a few buttons on my phone, why on earth wouldn't I?

Or consider the self-service checkout options that most grocery stores now offer. Consumers were skeptical about these at first, because not all the kinks had been worked out when the systems were first introduced. Now, you see lots of people using the self-service checkout facilities, and the lines move through those checkouts more quickly than they do through the traditional checkout lines. In addition, the kiosks in many stores are equipped with seamless, easy-to-use options that allow you to use in-store coupons, and even pay the grocery bill, just by using an app on your phone. If there's a problem with a product scan or with the kiosk, there's always an employee on hand ready to help the customer move the transaction forward. Again – if you can make your grocery trip that much quicker and easier by choosing the self-service option, why wouldn't you?

As this book goes to press, we are seeing self-checkout move from the "nice to have" category to the "table stakes" category. According to London-based research firm RBR, although the shift in consumer attitudes has been strengthened by changes in consumer preference patterns since the emergence of the global pandemic, it is part of a larger trend that was in play long before that. Alan Burt of RBR notes: "The COVID-19 crisis will only embolden long-standing and new self-checkout proponents alike to speed up expansion plans, with customers increasingly expecting such solutions as part of a wider array of checkout options."[4]

Notice that *both* of the self-service systems I have mentioned – airline bookings and grocery store checkouts – help customers to streamline processes that once used to involve a) waiting for a human being and b) carrying around pieces of paper. Notice, too, that both can now incorporate the act of downloading a company's app onto a smartphone to speed up the process even further. Grocery purchases and air travel are not the only examples of this, of course.

Many companies have come to the conclusion that creating powerful, effective self-service applications that customers can deploy from their phones is a powerful way to improve repeat-purchase numbers.

Self-service means more than offering alternatives to calling an agent for support, and it means more than offering a web page with FAQs. It means upping the game and enhancing the real-time level of personal control you give to the consumer.

Well-designed self-service options can create a whole new level of comfort and, as a result, a more positive, and more frequent, connection with customers. Giving customers the right self-service tools makes it easier for them to choose to make you part of their day – and then make that same choice again tomorrow.

The more confident a customer is that the self-service tools you offer will work, will get them where they want to go, and will be supported by real, live human beings when necessary, the more likely it is that the customer will think, *I like working with them. They always make it easy for me to do what I need to do!*

THE SIX CONVENIENCE PRINCIPLES

I should note briefly here that self-service is just one of the six convenience principles I wrote about in my book *The Convenience Revolution*. Here's a short rundown on all six.

Self-Service: Putting the customer in control of the process; giving the customer tools that allow them to control their own destiny... while at the same time offering them backup systems that enable them to connect to a human being if they so choose.

Technology: Using modern communications tools and platforms to make the customer feel more at home every time they interact with you.

Subscription: Automating the purchase process so that the customer gets what they need from you on a continuous basis. Not only does the customer say, "I'll be back" – they say, "I want to keep working with you indefinitely."

Delivery: Taking the product or service directly to the customer.

Access: Finding a way to answer the question, "Are you there when I need you?" with a yes.

Reducing Friction: Looking at the various points along the customer's journey that you can make a little easier. This is a never-ending process. This principle actually finds its way into all six principles; however, some companies focus on it, making it a major part of their value proposition. (It's so important that it's covered in detail in the next chapter of this book.)

When I wrote *The Convenience Revolution*, the whole idea of adding online self-service options was, in a lot of industries, optional. It was a disruptor in many industries, something you offered so you could stand out from the competition. Now it's everywhere. For instance, people are likely to wonder why their local gym doesn't offer a downloadable phone app or website option that allows them to reserve a training slot at a time that's perfect for them – and then track their results when they get to the gym. Lots of customers now expect that kind of app, so they may gravitate away from a gym that doesn't offer those options. The global pandemic of 2020 had a major impact on this trend, which was already gaining serious momentum. The various lockdowns people encountered all over the world put this trend on steroids. In many industries, letting customers do more to "call the shots" on their phone or computer is now much more of a "have to have" than a "nice to have."

The same goes for the other five convenience principles. How many people subscribed to a monthly service that delivered razor blades in the year 2010? How about dog food? How about prescription drugs? How many consider such a service to be a "built-in" part of their life today? Even though this phenomenon has been around for decades, the global pandemic that transformed commerce, and everything else, has dramatically accelerated customer expectations about convenience.

We want to be sure we're on the right side of the expectation curve. We'll explore this strategic imperative, and the critical concept of reducing friction, in much more depth in the next chapter.

KEY POINTS

- We are living in a culture of downloads, digital tools, and remote, self-paced purchasing.

- Giving more control to customers with self-service options is a great way to build loyalty.

- Be on the lookout for *new* ways to let customers choose what happens next.

- Self-service is not a destination. It's a direction.

- A good self-service option puts the customer in the driver's seat, *until and unless* they feel like asking for help with the driving.

- Creating powerful, effective self-service applications that customers can deploy using their phones may be a good way to improve repeat-purchase numbers.

- Self-Service is one of six core convenience principles that are revolutionizing customer service. The other five are: Technology, Subscription, Delivery, Access, and Reducing Friction.

CONVERSATION STARTERS

- What is your favorite online retailer? Why?
- How would you describe that online retailer's self-service tools? How much of the experience do you control? How easy is it for you to get help from a human being if you need it?
- What could your organization adapt or implement, using that online retailer's self-service resources as an example?

TAKE ACTION!

Set up a team to review your organization's self-service offerings for its customers, and task it with making recommendations for improvements.

NOTES

1. Source: *The Value of Customer Self-Service in the Digital Age*, Toma Kulbyte, October 20, 2020, https://www.superoffice .com/blog/customer-self-service/.

2. Source: Dimension Data study.

3. Source: "U.S. air passengers' preferred channels to book flights in 2017, by category" https://www.statista.com/ statistics/539774/airline-travelers-methods-booking-tickets/.

4. Source: "What's Next for Food Retail Self-Checkout?" https://progressivegrocer.com/whats-next-food-retail-self -checkout.

CHAPTER 12

NO FRICTION, PLEASE

One of the points I hope you picked up in the previous chapter is this:

> When it comes to convenience, there is only one constant: Customers expect more of it, and they expect it on a regular basis.

So, just to recap: You see this pattern play out again and again. Some convenience that was optional for companies yesterday is no longer optional. It has become part of the customer's basic requirements. And the convenience that is optional today will be considered standard tomorrow. This cycle has always been with us, but in the twenty-first century, we see it accelerating just about everywhere.

Guess what? That same basic dynamic holds true for all six of the convenience principles I shared with you in the previous chapter. All six of them are growing exponentially in both importance and impact as you read these words. When it comes to building and sustaining relationships with customers, you want to be familiar with all six. But there is one in particular I want to focus on, a principle that is especially important for any team, in any industry, that is focused on customer loyalty. It's the last one I shared with you – *removing friction*. And it underlies the other five items on the list.

Removing friction simply means making processes more hassle-free for the customer.

This is a job that's never finished, and that's good news, at least for companies that are interested in securing repeat business and creating Moments of Magic. The fact that we're never done removing friction means we always have an opportunity to make things better for our customers – and always have an opportunity to create an emotional connection with them.

Today, removing friction is far more than just a competitive differentiator – it's a strategic imperative. If you *don't* do it consistently, and if you *don't* get feedback from your customers regularly about how well you're doing it, you will find yourself behind the curve. Here's why:

> # When everything else is equal, the company that becomes *steadily more* convenient has the edge in the never-ending battle for repeat business and customer loyalty.

THE FRICTION REDUCTION CYCLE

Here's an important insight into reducing friction: We don't want to get too complacent about any single incident of friction that we're fortunate enough to be able to remove for our customers. Why? Because every breakthrough in this area is passing; every new instance of friction reduced is part of a cycle. Any given breakthrough when it comes to creating new levels of hassle-free operation for the customer doesn't stay a breakthrough for long. To the contrary, it quickly becomes second nature for both us and the customer, following this easy-to-predict Friction Reduction Cycle:

Let's look a little more closely at each of these terms. They're extremely important to understand. We don't want to get them mixed up.

WHAT IS A BREAKTHROUGH?

Every time we find a new way to reduce friction in the customer's world, that's a *breakthrough*.

I'll give you one of my favorite examples of a friction-reduction breakthrough. On June 27, 1967, the British bank Barclays unveiled a novelty: cash dispensing machines, also known as automatic teller machines, or ATMs. The first six of these machines, the brainchild of a team led by the Scottish inventor John Shepherd-Barron, opened to the public on that day.

Prior to June 27, 1967, if you wanted to withdraw cash from your bank, you had to wait until the bank was open and then wait in line behind a lot of people, many of whom had other kinds of business to do with the bank. Very often, the line moved quite slowly. Now, with Barclays' technical innovation, customers who wanted to withdraw cash could do so at any hour of the day or night. They often had little or no wait time, as customers in front of them completed ATM transactions quickly. Friction removed! Suddenly there was a whole new level of convenience experienced by Barclays' customers.

> **Any time we remove an obstacle that is preventing customers from getting through their day in the easiest, most trouble-free way, we are *removing friction*.**

Breakthroughs in friction reduction are advances that remove obstacles people had long imagined were simply part of everyday life. For Barclays' customers in 1967, those first six ATMs were not just technological advancements, they were above-average experiences that transformed their whole relationship with the bank. They were breakthroughs.

Yet there is something vitally important that we need to notice about removing friction: It's only perceived as an above-average experience – a Moment of Magic – when customers don't take the convenience for granted. The process by which we take convenience for granted is often very rapid indeed. Convenience, like technology and communications, is not a static experience. When customers figure out that a new level of convenience is available, they gravitate toward it, and that sets up ripples in the marketplace.

WHAT IS A TREND?

Very often, breakthroughs are pursued by multiple players simultaneously. Just nine days after Barclays gave their customers access to the new cash dispensing machines, a bank in Sweden unveiled a similar system, and within two years a much more sophisticated online cash dispensing system, developed by Burroughs, became widely available to banking customers in the United States.

Now ATMs were a clear *trend*. Some companies offered them. Others didn't. But it was increasingly obvious in which direction customers wanted to go. Each time a company raised its game by giving its customers access to the new way of banking, they gained a competitive edge. Fast-moving banks picked up on the trend and built better relationships with their customers as a result;

slower-moving banks who failed to fall in line with the trend ran the risk of seeming inconvenient in comparison. Guess what? They *were* less convenient than the competition. And that's not a good place to be.

WHAT IS AN EXPECTATION?

Fast-forward to today. It's estimated that there are three million functioning cash machines worldwide. ATMs are how most of us now come into contact with physical currency – and a bank that claims to serve on-the-go customers and doesn't offer some kind of ATM access isn't going to last very long in the marketplace. ATMs are now an *expectation*. If, for some reason, the bank you choose to use has a technical glitch that takes down all its ATMs for an extended period, you will notice... and you might start thinking about whether it makes sense to look for another bank.

Any given example of reduced friction starts out as a breakthrough that makes the customer's journey easier. If the breakthrough delivers lasting convenience to the customer, you can expect it to become a trend in your market.

Eventually, a trend becomes an expectation – something that anyone and everyone who aims to serve the customer should be prepared to deliver.

A KEY QUESTION: ARE YOU MEETING EXPECTATIONS... OR CREATING FRICTION?

Although it's great to create breakthroughs, it's also incredibly important to be sure that you're meeting current customer expectations when it comes to minimizing friction. You don't want to be the last bank in town wondering whether it's a good idea to bring in one of those newfangled ATMs everyone is talking about. Make no mistake: If you *are* that bank, you may wake up one morning and wonder why all the customers are making their deposits and withdrawals somewhere else.

We cannot expect to win loyalty from our customers if there's built-in friction in our offering that our competitors have already gotten rid of. Take a close look at your customer experience and ask yourself: What activities and processes add needless friction to the customer's world? What friction could you remove from the customer experience in order to keep customers from drifting over to the competition?

To get you started, here is my list of ten ways that companies (and employees) typically create friction for their customers. Even one of these is a loyalty killer. These are the "convenience infractions" that drive away customers. If you want them to keep coming back for more, you will find a way to remove *all* these events from your customer's radar screen.

1. Bad Policies

As a customer, don't you hate it when someone does something that seems like a waste of your time, or puts up a needless obstacle to you getting what you're after – and then blames it on a policy they supposedly have no control over? Don't you hate it when a service provider gives you an instant negative response to a question and then says, "It's company policy," as though that explains everything? News flash: That kind of response doesn't explain anything. If there is a guideline we have no choice but to follow, it's our job to explain to the customer *why* the guideline is there, *how* it's relevant to the present situation, and *what* the alternate plan of action is for getting the customer closer to where he or she wants to be. And by the way, if a particular rule keeps coming up as an example of friction in our customer's world, we need to find a way to change it.

2. Duplicate Paperwork

I'm always amazed at the amount of duplicate paperwork and online forms that customers are asked to fill out. Many of the leaders I work with are aware that this is a big problem when it comes to holding on to customers. These leaders have set up teams tasked with finding ways to reduce the amount of duplicate paperwork. If your organization needs to launch such a team, start the discussion about how this launch should happen.

3. Cumbersome Technology

Hard-to-navigate websites and apps drive away customers. Period. Many companies have no idea how cumbersome their technology is for the customer, because they haven't recently – or ever – given the technology a test drive. If you haven't recently tried to use your website or app in the way a customer would use it, do so. If the tech needs to be upgraded, upgrade it.

4. Broken Anything

If something is broken, start fixing it the moment you find out about it. Customers can't be expected to keep doing business with companies that don't make important repairs within a reasonable period of time.

5. Making Customers Wait

Sometimes a wait is inevitable. Customers understand that. However, if you find yourself in a situation where you have to make a customer wait, let them know how long the wait is going to be. Then don't be late!

6. Inconsistent Information

When a customer gets two or more different answers to the same question, what do you think happens? Confusion! Confusion is not just pain you cause in the customer's brain. Confusion is friction that can motivate your customers to defect to the competition.

7. Poorly Trained Employees

When people have not been trained properly for the role they're supposed to fulfill, it damages our relationship with the customer and makes it harder for the customer to trust us in the future. Who's to say that they won't have the same experience with a similarly under-trained employee the next time around? Employees who demonstrate a lack of knowledge or competency frustrate customers. And frustration is friction.

8. Not Being Able to Talk to a Person

There is a generational component to this one. Younger customers may feel less of a need to connect voice to voice, in real time, in order to get a problem or issue solved,[1] and they may be more inclined to use self-service resources. But *everybody* eventually reaches a point where they want to talk to someone voice to voice about a service issue. It's our job to make that happen as seamlessly and easily as possible. When customers have a hard time tracking down a real, live human being to talk to (or text with, if that's the only option), they get frustrated. Some companies make it way too difficult to get to a human being.

9. A Bad Customer Experience Design

Is the experience your customer has with your company the result of conscious design? Or did it happen randomly, as the result of internal decisions and discussions that didn't take the customer into account? Companies are now assigning executive titles to the person in charge of "CX design." This has nothing to do with designing labels and packaging and graphics; this is about designing the total end-to-end experience the customer has with your company. This is the person who is in charge of eliminating friction. If your company doesn't have such a person, that needs to change – whatever title the person holds.

10. Anything That Wastes a Customer's Time

This is more than the dreaded "long hold" in a customer support call. This is about making a conscious effort to save the customer time. Anything that doesn't save the customer time, or wastes their valuable time, is friction.

This isn't meant to be a rant. It's simply a list of some of the ways companies frustrate their customers and cause friction. It's only a partial list, but it's a start.

Remember, not meeting a customer expectation puts us at a major disadvantage in the marketplace. Don't imagine you can paper over a friction problem or "coast" on breakthroughs that happened weeks, months, years, or even decades ago. If you want to deliver the consistently above-average experiences that make customers think, *It's* ***always*** *so easy to work with them!* you must be continually on the lookout for ways to remove friction from your customer's world.

Reducing friction is a way of running a business. It's not a one-time activity. Rest assured that, even if you're not focused on looking for new ways to reduce friction for your customer, *your competition is!*

Can new technologies help us remove friction from the customer experience? Absolutely! But technology alone is not the answer. In the next chapter, we'll examine the limits of automation as a tool for improving customer loyalty.

KEY POINTS

- Any time we remove an obstacle that is preventing customers from getting through their day in the easiest, most trouble-free way, we are *removing friction.*

- Any breakthrough in reducing friction doesn't stay a breakthrough for long. It quickly becomes a trend.

- Trends eventually become expectations – something that anyone and everyone who aims to serve customers should be prepared to deliver on.

- Ten common ways companies (and employees) create friction for their customers are:

  1. Bad policies.
  2. Duplicate paperwork.
  3. Cumbersome technology.
  4. Broken anything.
  5. Making customers wait.
  6. Inconsistent information.
  7. Poorly trained employees.
  8. Not being able to talk to a person.
  9. A bad customer-experience design.
  10. Anything that wastes a customer's time.

- Removing friction is a never-ending job.

CONVERSATION STARTERS

- Is your organization guilty of any of the convenience infractions that showed up in this chapter? Are you adding needless friction that could push your customers over to the competition? If so, how can you remove it?

- What kind of friction is your organization creating for employees? (Remember, whenever you create friction for employees, it usually results in some form of friction for the customer.) How can that friction be removed?

- How can you seek, develop, and create breakthroughs that reduce friction and raise the bar on the customer experience?

TAKE ACTION!

Identify one specific piece of friction that shows up in your organization's customer experience. Then find a way to remove it!

NOTE

1.   Source: 2020 Achieving Customer Amazement Survey. https://hyken.com/2020aca.

CHAPTER 13

YOU CAN'T AUTOMATE A RELATIONSHIP

Do you treat your customers like human beings or like account numbers? Does a customer feel like a person during interactions with your company or like a transaction?

These are important questions. If you're serious about creating the kind of experience that predictably turns one-time customers into repeat customers, and repeat customers into loyal customers, you'll have to conduct a special kind of analysis. You'll have to take a close look at how well you and your organization are doing when it comes to building an emotional and/or a human-to-human connection as part of your customer's experience.

This is non-negotiable. Whether your customer shows up in person, you show up at the customer's doorstep, everything happens remotely via the Internet, or there is some hybrid of those approaches, you will want to conduct this kind of evaluation.

> # The human touch, or at least a convincing evocation of it, is essential to creating customer loyalty. This is true even if – especially if – you never connect in person with the customer.

THE HUMAN TOUCH TARGET

No matter how advanced our communication tools may become, no matter how much flexibility and autonomy we give our customers in the self-service options we offer, no matter how conversant our customer base may be with cutting-edge technology, there is still room for us to improve when it comes to connecting, as one human being to another, with an individual customer. That improvement should be ongoing. It should be something the customer notices and remembers. It does not have to cost us a great deal of money, nor does it have to take up massive amounts of our planning time. But it needs to happen.

Fortunately, making it happen can be a lot of fun. If we do this right, we can have a blast identifying new ways to build meaningful, enjoyable human contact into the customer's experience with our organization. I call this the Human Touch Target, and I believe fulfilling that target should become a regular process built into your plan. The frequency of this contact will depend on your industry, your business, and the degree to which your customer expects you to stay in touch on a personal basis – but with very rare exceptions (and I'll deal with those in a moment), you will want to set specific goals for creating this kind of personal contact. Why in the world would you want a customer to go a long time without experiencing any kind of human touch with your company?

IF YOU ARE LOOKING FOR
AN EASY WAY TO GET STARTED...

Here's the simplest, most obvious, most impactful, and easiest-to-implement example of a Human Touch I can think of: a personalized handwritten note. This is great for salespeople and for any number of industries, including retail, hospitality, and professional services, among others.

This message could be a thank-you note to your very best customers, or it could be an acknowledgment of almost any occasion in the customer's life, such as an anniversary, a birthday, or a professional accomplishment. It could even be a letter you write for no reason other than to express your gratitude for the opportunity to work with that person. All that has to happen is that the letter shows your customer you are thinking of them. At my company, we do this on a regular basis to let our customers know just how important they are to us.

In case you were wondering, emails and text messages don't count for this particular Human Touch. There's nothing wrong with reaching out to a customer in those ways, of course, but let's face it, they don't have the emotional impact of a physical, personalized letter. This particular exercise is about putting pen to paper and expressing your authentic feelings to that customer. Surely your most important customers are worth this minimal investment of time, attention, paper, ink, and postage!

This particular variety of Human Touch communication has a powerful impact in our digital age. Think about it. Our customers get hundreds of texts and emails, and they delete the vast majority of them instantly. It's a real event, one worthy of notice, when they receive a handwritten letter from anyone! When they do, and when that letter focuses on something positive like gratitude, how do you think customers feel? Noticed. Acknowledged. Validated. Valued. You can expect them to read such handwritten messages more than once and to share their contents with others. They may well keep them indefinitely! Why on earth wouldn't you reach out and make that kind of experience happen with your very best customers – or with brand-new customers whom you want to turn into repeat customers?

THE RELATIONSHIP IS WHAT COUNTS

Why bother with the Human Touch? Isn't it more convenient to send out an email blast that says thank you to hundreds of people at a time, using a message that's identical, or only slightly personalized? Taking this approach may be more convenient for us, and it may connect to a process or system we already have in place, but it doesn't do anything to improve our relationship with a given customer. Why not? Because customers are already inundated with email messages. How inundated? Sometimes, we find that even if we do go to the trouble of writing and sending a unique email message, the customer assumes that it's part of a digital mass mailing! We need to look beyond familiar processes and systems and start thinking about how to support the relationship.

You can automate a process, but you can't automate a human relationship.

The greatest technology in the world hasn't replaced the ultimate relationship tool between a customer and the business: one-on-one communication. That's what makes the most powerful emotional connection with a customer. And that's what the Human Touch is all about.

A regular Human Touch allows you to create a true relationship with your customer. Once we start connecting with customers as human beings, whether that's in person or through some remote communication strategy – whether it's by a Zoom call, a shared cup of coffee, or a holiday card featuring a personalized message – the interaction takes on a depth and meaning that it didn't have before.

We all like the human touch. We all seek it out and respond well to it as customers. And we all need to realize that it's what our customers want from us, whether they say it out loud or not. (Usually, they don't!)

THE BIG CHALLENGE THAT COMPANIES FACE

The human touch seems, in recent years, to be in increasingly short supply. While doing research for this book, I came across a quote that is popularly – and, I eventually confirmed, inaccurately – attributed to Albert Einstein. It really doesn't matter who actually said it, but whoever it was, they hit the nail on the head in describing the major challenge companies faced in the first half of the twentieth century:

> **"I fear the day that technology will surpass our human interaction. The world will have a generation of idiots."**

You may not agree with that prediction, but whether you do or not, I hope you see how it illuminates a task we all face of getting customers to want to do business with us again and again. A lot of companies today seem committed to designing a customer experience that eliminates human interaction altogether! Fortunately, we're not quite there yet. And there's still time to adjust. You can make that adjustment with the handwritten letter technique and also by the following means:

- Reaching out by phone to important customers with no appointment. Yes, you can do this just to check in and see how they are, how things are going in their world, and what they'd like to see improved on your side. There's no law saying that the customer always has to be the one who calls us! We can initiate contact with the customer, and we don't have to wait for a problem or issue to do that.

- Scheduling a monthly or quarterly review meeting. This should be second nature with your most important customers. If they're worth holding on to, they're worth scheduling a half-hour meeting with, to get feedback on what's working... and what isn't.

- Setting up a special customer appreciation event. This can take any number of forms, depending on your business model and your customers' preferences and routines. Just make sure the event is fun, focused on the customers, and friction-free. Don't try to sell anything during these events. Just make sure customers feel appreciated and noticed.

Don't get me wrong. Digital is okay. In fact, digital is great! But there must be a balance. There is nothing wrong with building your company around a great digital and online experience. But as I pointed out elsewhere in this book, there must always be the option of a seamless hand-off to a real, live human when the customer needs one.

And by the way, if for some reason you have to make a customer wait for that human contact, you may want to consider injecting a dose of humor into the messaging, to remind customers that there really are people on both sides of the interaction. Is this approach right for every company and every brand? No. Can it serve as an inspiration for companies looking for new ways to humanize the customer experience? Absolutely!

One of my all-time favorite examples of a company that did this is San Diego-based Barnstorming Adventures, which provides rides on vintage airplanes. If you happen to call them on their 800 line and an employee couldn't be there to take your call, here is what you would hear: "All our lines are busy, but your call is very important to us. Blah, blah, blah. (Pause.) Why is it companies say your call is important but then don't answer the darn phone? Well, we tried to find a better solution, but we're a small company, and sometimes we just can't do everything at once. Right now, we're busier than a one-armed wing-walker with a wedgie, but we'll be with you just as soon as we get our feet on the ground."

This is a great example of a pre-written, pre-recorded non-human communication that takes what would otherwise be a Moment of Mediocrity... and turns it into a Moment of Magic by leveraging a classic human bonding experience: shared laughter. If it makes sense for your company and your culture, consider giving this a try.

THE SEEMINGLY HUMAN-FREE LOYALTY EXPERIENCE

Let's acknowledge that some companies have done extremely well and created truly extraordinary customer loyalty, while at the same time building a customer experience that is seemingly 100 percent digital—meaning that for most customers, most of the time, there is never the need, or even the desire, to connect with a human being at all. (But do notice that word "seemingly." I'll be coming back to it later.)

When I ask people to identify a company that they love coming back to again and again without having to, or wanting to, interact with an actual human being, Amazon always seems to head the list. This is one of the reasons it's virtually impossible to write a book about contemporary customer service and customer experience without at least mentioning Amazon. I've written about the company at length in the past; I'll share a few brief observations on their strategy for building loyalty now.

Improving the customer retention rate by just a few percentage points can have a massive positive impact on an organization's profitability, and it's a good bet that Amazon founder Jeff Bezos is aware of this fact. Generating high levels of customer retention is a major component of Amazon's business strategy. Consider that, in retail, a retention rate of above 60 percent is generally considered good. Amazon's customer retention rate is a jaw-dropping 90 percent.[1]

How has Amazon accomplished the remarkable level of repeat business and loyalty they enjoy?

There are many possible answers to that question, but the extraordinary level of customer loyalty Amazon has achieved surely has something to do with a digital experience that is so intuitive that it usually feels like the customer is interacting with a human being – and a very knowledgeable one at that. That's why the Amazon customer becomes steadily more confident in their relationship with the company. And that confidence, combined with friction-free subscription services such as Amazon Prime that support the retail experience, is why customers keep coming back for more.

One of the biggest weapons in Amazon's confidence-creation arsenal is a consistent, intuitive ease of use that lets the customer feel "at home" when they visit the site. Without that foundation of convenience, the repeat business, and the quality of the typical customer's relationship with the company, would not be as impressive. This is a high bar. Most companies do not meet the Amazon standard for ease of use online.

Amazon also creates confidence through a powerful AI-driven recommendation engine that highlights products of interest to a specific consumer with remarkable accuracy. This feature is so glove-fitting, so reliable, so good at remembering what you did in the past, and so accurate at forecasting what you might want to consider in the future, that it's roughly equivalent to a conversation with a real, and well-trained, human employee. It's as though you're always in discussion with the company on the following subject: "What else do you think I might like?" – and always getting good information back. Again, this is something Amazon invests heavily in and does better at than its competitors.

As if that weren't enough, the company creates confidence with their ability to communicate effectively, accurately, and reliably with the customer about exactly what's been ordered and shipped. Amazon customers have grown used to features like instant acknowledgment of the order, messaging about when the item has actually left the warehouse and when it will arrive, and comprehensive but easy-to-understand shipping updates complete with tracking information and "Where is it now" status checks. In some cases, they even give you a picture of the item being left at your doorstep! And let's not forget that Amazon's inventory management and shipping processes are cutting-edge, operate on a massive scale and, in the vast majority of cases, create little or no friction in the customer ordering experience.

Creating and sustaining the kind of infrastructure necessary to consistently deliver this level of confidence in the digital process is not easy, and not all companies can make the human and financial investments necessary to make it happen. What I want you to notice, though, is that there are things that Amazon does that you definitely can do. Amazon continually adds value to the customer's world in two critical ways: first, by constantly upgrading and streamlining that digital experience and removing friction; and second, by making sure there's always a human contact option if the customer, for whatever reason, decides they need it.

Here is where that all-important word "seemingly" comes into play. Although the experience may seem 100 percent digital, it isn't. Even Amazon doesn't rely entirely on algorithms and digital tools to deliver the customer experience. Yes, they have designed a platform that is so intuitive, so comprehensive, and so friction-free that it doesn't usually require the human backup to come into play. But make no mistake, it's there when Amazon customers need it.

THREE REALITY CHECKS

Here are three essential reality checks we need to give ourselves when it comes to evaluating our customer service experience for the Human Touch.

Reality Check #1:
Leaders who focus on tech at the expense of human relationships needlessly distance themselves from customers.

As has already been mentioned in this chapter, this is a serious competitive disadvantage. If you are looking for a way to ensure your best customers begin to seriously consider your competition, here's one of the best strategies for doing that: Make it hard for them to connect with your people. Note that to drive your customers away, you don't have to make it impossible to do business with you, you just have to make it a hassle. You have to create friction. And remember, unless you sell something the customer can't get anywhere else, creating a business model with zero potential for human interaction puts your company at risk of becoming a commodity, with no differentiation between you and the competitor. The Human Touch is a powerful differentiator.

Reality Check #2:
Technology should not be 100 percent of the experience.

If we're aiming to create a relationship with a loyal customer, and we should be, then we need to recognize that technology can only go so far; it's in our interest to give the customer the option of a human connection. If they want access to a human being to solve a problem or handle an unexpected situation, we should give them that access. Technology alone may be able to create a repeat customer, but for most companies, it's unlikely to create a loyal customer. One of the best ways of making that loyalty happen is to connect the customer to another human being. Our goal should be to consciously design that Human Touch into the experience in a way that makes financial and logistical sense and complements our technology.

Reality Check #3:
Not all of our customers will respond to technology in the same way – a fact that gives us an invaluable opportunity to build a human connection.

As has already been pointed out, there are major generational issues here. People born before 1965 are likely to be most receptive to a "human touch," with real-time voice-to-voice or face-to-face interactions. That's what they grew up with. That's what they've come to expect. For many of them, that's what a human connection is. We are well advised to give these customers ways of connecting with us that leverage phone calls or any other direct human-to-human communication, including video conferencing. Broadly speaking, customers who are born after 1965 are likely to be more receptive to person-to-person communication that takes the form of chat sessions, text messages, or other digital interactions. Notice, this does not mean they like receiving messages from robots! While robots and automated messages can play a part when needed, there still needs to be a human being on the other end of the conversation, someone responding authentically and with appropriate emotion. Here is the big takeaway when it comes to the Human Touch:

Provide options that allow people to engage with you in the way that feels most human to them.

In the next chapter, we'll look at why customers stop doing business with your organization... and when you should stop doing business with a customer.

KEY POINTS

- You can automate a process, but you can't automate a human relationship.

- Leaders who focus on tech at the expense of human relationships needlessly distance themselves from customers.

- Technology should not be 100 percent of the experience.

- Not all of our customers will respond to technology in the same way – a fact that gives us an invaluable opportunity to build a human connection.

- Provide options that allow people to engage with you in the way that feels most human to them.

CONVERSATION STARTERS

- Name a company that you have had a positive Human Touch connection with. Describe what happened to make you feel that way.

- When was the last time you had a real-time, person-to-person discussion with a customer?

- Do you think the customer felt an emotional connection with your organization during that conversation? Why or why not?

- How often should a customer experience a Human Touch interaction with your company?

TAKE ACTION!

Identify at least one amazing Human Touch interaction you could have with a customer that you aren't making happen now. Then... make it happen!

NOTE

1. Source: "How Amazon maintains over 90% customer retention," https://www.getbeamer.com/blog/how -amazon-maintains-over-90-customer-retention-year -over-year#:~:text=As%20of%20June%202019%2C%20 Amazon,and%2098%25%20after%20two%20years.

CHAPTER 14

YOU'RE TERMINATED!

They used to be your customer.

Then you lost them to the competition. Why?

Below, you will find ten reasons customers choose to terminate their relationships with companies like yours... and never come back. Read all ten of them closely. Study them. Understand them. Don't let them happen in your world!

TEN LIKELY REASONS YOUR CUSTOMER TERMINATED YOU

Reason #1:
Apathy

Maybe they left because there was no connection, no emotional investment, and no relationship between you worthy of the name. Somewhere along the line, you forgot: The customer is not an account number or just another sale, but a person with unique experiences, wants, needs, desires, and emotions. The customer is a human being, just like you. As a human being, the customer likes to connect with other people. You had a chance to connect with them, but none of your people took advantage of that chance. As a result, there was no reason for them to do business with you again... and no reason for them not to start working with someone else when the opportunity arose to do so. You acted like you didn't care, and the customer did the same in return.

Reason #2:
Rudeness

It's not how you like to think of your organization, but it's got to be said: It's possible that the person on your team with whom your customer interacted was so disrespectful that the customer decided they'd had enough. Someone on your team may have been adversarial. They didn't treat the customer like they mattered. They treated the customer like an interruption. They said things they shouldn't have said. Don't bother trying to explain that the customer happened to reach someone who was having a bad day, or that other people on your team have a better attitude, or that what happened isn't what usually happens. It's the weakest link in the chain that determines whether or not the chain holds strong – or snaps. In this case, it snapped. Accept that! The customer's image of your entire organization was formed in the moment that one person on your team was rude. And guess what? It's a good bet that your customer will be sharing that experience, and their perceptions of your organization, with friends, relatives, and work colleagues. And not just in person. They might even decide to take this online.

Beware: Rudeness has a way of going viral.

Reason #3:
Your contact information wasn't easily accessible.

When the customer had a problem or issue, they had to go hunting through different pages on your website to track down contact information you should have given them easy access to from the start. You frustrated them. Frustration is friction. So, what happened? Even if you were eventually able to solve the problem or answer the question, the customer's main emotional memory of interacting with your organization was friction. They gave up and went to the competition, simply because it was easier to connect with them. It didn't have to be that way.

Reason #4:
They couldn't connect with you on the channel they prefer using.

News flash: The customer is an individual. You forgot that channel preference is incredibly important to individual consumers, and you forgot that channel preference is hugely influenced by the generation the customer belongs to. So, if this was an older customer who prefers interacting with people in real time, but you didn't have any option available for them to do that – even as a backup – what you were saying was that you weren't interested in talking to them at all. By the same token, if this was a younger customer, and you didn't make it easy for them to text or email you, you were sending the same negative message: that you simply didn't care about connecting. You didn't make it easy (or possible) for people to interact with you using the platform they felt most at home using. Surprise, surprise: When people don't feel at home, they don't make repeat purchases.

Reason #5:
You simply didn't respond when they told you they had a problem.

The customer raised an issue with you, but then heard nothing back. Their communication with you fell into a black hole. From your perspective, this may look like a system problem, a process issue that you need to analyze, troubleshoot, and resolve, so it doesn't happen again. But you know what? From the customer's perspective, it has nothing to do with systems and processes. It's a relationship problem. They tried to talk to you about something that was important to them, and they heard nothing back. There was no effort to repair the damage, so they decided that you just didn't care and opted to work with someone else.

Reason #6:
You had a poor response time.

The customer left a message, and you didn't get back to them within a reasonable period of time. When you finally did reach out, hours, days, or even weeks after they had first contacted you, they felt frustrated – whether they said that out loud or not. (By the way, the fact that they didn't say anything to you about any of these problems does not let you off the hook.) No matter what happened after that long delay, it was hard for them to get excited about working with your organization again, because they assumed your poor response time reflected your attitude toward other things – like quality. So, when the opportunity presented itself to work with someone else, they moved on.

Reason #7:
They had a problem, and you responded, but you didn't make an effort.

Even if you couldn't give the customer exactly what they wanted, you could have connected with them in a way that made them feel you were giving it an honest try. Customers don't expect perfection from every interaction. They know there are going to be bumps in the road from time to time. But when they invested the time, effort, and energy to ask for help in resolving a problem they were having with your product or service, you didn't reciprocate by trying to make them feel great about working with you. Maybe one of your team members recited the rulebook instead of expressing empathy for the challenges they were experiencing. Maybe you failed to even acknowledge that there was a problem. The point is, the customer felt slighted, didn't feel listened to, and didn't feel like they had a partner. You lost sight of the fact that every Moment of Misery, without exception, presents you with an opportunity to create a Moment of Magic in their world. And as a result, you left the Moment of Misery as the defining experience of working with you. So, the customer decided they'd had enough.

Reason #8:
You made them wait too darn long.

If you put the customer on hold for two hours, don't be surprised if they don't want to come back and do business with you again. Am I exaggerating? Maybe. But somewhere along the line, you forgot that a ten- or twenty-minute hold time felt like two hours to the customer. Customers realize that sometimes they may have to be put on hold, but they also know there's a better way to do it. It's the twenty-first century, and there are technology options you could have considered or put into play. There's really no excuse for not letting the customer know how long the wait will be, not offering them an option to have a call-back on a timeline that works for both of you, or not giving them a chance to let you know when they'll be available to talk. You didn't do any of that. So, they got frustrated (there's that friction again) and lost patience. Why would they want to do business with you if they have to go through that kind of time-wasting exercise, not to mention the stress it causes? Why would they want their next issue or question addressed with the same level of disregard for their time?

Reason #9:
You made them repeat the same story again and again.

The customer kept getting switched from one person to the next. Each time, they had to start over and explain the issue all over again. Even worse, they got different answers from different people each time they told their story. There are lots of companies, big and small, in all kinds of industries, that have figured out how to avoid making customers repeat their story again and again when they have to talk to different customer service representatives. Someone needs to create a better system for your organization, and eventually you may find a way to figure that out, but in the meantime, the customer is not willing to wait around for you to sort out the problems.

Reason #10:
Somebody else listened when you wouldn't.

When the customer explained to you what the issue was, they got a sense that you weren't really there. You seemed too busy, too tired, or (if the customer was calling a support center) too fixated on your own prewritten script to even process the customer's question, much less respond creatively to it. That caused a Moment of Misery, and although that moment was something you could have capitalized on – perhaps by changing course in the conversation, perhaps by putting the customer in touch with a different team member – you didn't do that. You let the Moment of Misery stand. This meant that the customer had no good reason to stick around. When the opportunity arose to work with another company that had people who were better at listening to them, they decided to work with that company instead.

If any one of these ten reasons sounds familiar, or even possible, for customers who interact with your organization, you now know why you got terminated. Of course, there are plenty of other reasons they could have decided to move on. Those are just some of the most common.

Notice that none of the ten reasons you just read about has anything to do with price or service quality. If you had been competitive and consistent in each of these ten areas, you would have kept the customer from even comparing prices, service plans, and product specs with your competition. But you didn't... so they left.

And here's a bonus eleventh reason to consider: There was nothing above average for the customer to point to when the competition came knocking. So, someone new showed up and they decided to give them a shot – not because of any negative experience they had with you, but because the experience wasn't really positive, either. Maybe they went over to the competition because you performed to only the minimum acceptable standard. You don't have to deliver a *bad* experience for this to happen. All you have to do is deliver a consistently *mediocre* experience.

WHEN SHOULD YOU TERMINATE A CUSTOMER?

Of course, we should look at the flip side, too. Are there situations where it makes sense for you to terminate a relationship with a customer? It's certainly possible. Here are three reasons to consider (tactfully) terminating the relationship:

Reason #1:
You weren't able to meet the customer's expectations and don't think you can.

Despite repeated, good-faith attempts on your side to make it work, you have not been able to make them happy. Note that just categorizing someone as a "difficult customer" after a single tense exchange does not qualify as a good-faith attempt to make the relationship work. What does? Well, usually we're talking about a situation where you're trying, over an extended period of time, to take care of the customer, you're doing the very best you can, and they're just not happy with anything you've been able to give them. You've even asked them what you can do to make them happy, and based on the answer you received, you know you cannot deliver on what they want. This is the point where it makes sense to politely and helpfully say something like the following: "Hey, I'm really sorry we haven't been able to get you where you want to go, but let me give you the names of some people who might be able to help you out." Bear in mind, though, that many so-called "difficult customers" are challenging you and your organization to live up to a higher standard. Examine the situation closely before you decide that you're not willing to live up to that standard.

Reason #2:
The customer is unacceptably rude to a team member.

Yes, it may be necessary to move on in this situation. Just make sure you have a clear sense of what caused the rudeness. If there are relevant call recordings, or chat and email transcripts, review them to confirm there are no issues on your side that caused the customer to react in an extreme way. Once you are certain of that, take action. Standing up for your team members when a customer is unacceptably rude demonstrates your commitment and care toward your own people. That's incredibly important, because the way your employees are treated determines how customers are going to be treated! Maintaining a strong sense that your employees have a safe place to work and will be protected is more important than a single transaction with a single rude customer.

Reason #3:
The customer has not paid bills.

If you're not getting paid, it doesn't make business sense to continue the relationship. Do what you can to make the relationship work. Show empathy. Try to work together to address the issue. It's important for you to understand why the payments are not being made before you close out the relationship. The customer may be going through a tough time, and if that's the case, you will want to find out all the details. You may be able to set up a repayment plan that works for both sides. At some point, though, you may need to conclude that it's time to cut the line and move on.

Even when you do choose to close out the relationship for the foreseeable future, bear in mind that it doesn't have to be forever.

Terminating a relationship with a customer doesn't mean you wouldn't want them to come back under better circumstances.

In most cases, you will want to keep the door cracked open – so you can return in a few weeks or months, check in, and find out what's going on in the person's world. It may make sense to work together again... and even if it doesn't, the person may have referrals for you to follow up on.

One final cautionary note: It is important that management is actively involved in any decision to terminate a relationship with a given customer. Even though we want to empower people to make good decisions, some decisions should get a manager's or leader's review. This prevents such decisions from being made too quickly, or without appropriate review of all the relevant facts. This is a big decision, and it's one we want to be sure to get right. Customer-facing team members should have access to support, advice, and guidance before the decision is made to cut ties with a customer. If that decision to cut ties is made, management will want to suggest the best ways to ensure the door remains open to do business in the future. We always want team members to be focused on serving the customer; the decision to part ways points in the opposite direction, so it's essential that someone from management signs off on it.

In the next chapter, we'll connect all the dots... and start creating a powerful "I'll Be Back" experience for your customers.

KEY POINTS

- Customers may leave because there's no connection, no emotional investment, and no relationship with our organization.

- Rudeness has a way of going viral. Sometimes, customers give up and go to the competition simply because it's easier to get in touch with them.

- Customers may also terminate us because:

  - We don't make it easy for them to connect with us on the platform they prefer.

  - We make them repeat their problems multiple times.

  - We take too long to resolve their issues.

- Terminating a relationship with a customer doesn't mean we don't want them back under better circumstances.

- Customer-facing team members deserve support, advice, and guidance in deciding to cut ties with a customer.

CONVERSATION STARTERS

- Think of a specific customer your company lost – and shouldn't have. Why did that person leave?

- Are there any other reasons, beyond the ones on this list, that might cause a customer in your world to say, "You're terminated"? If so, what are they?

- When does it make sense, in your world, to terminate a customer? How is management involved in this decision?

TAKE ACTION!

Do a termination self-check with your team. This important process has three steps:

Step One

Closely review all ten of the reasons a customer might terminate a relationship with your organization, or any new ones you have uncovered, and discuss them in depth with the entire team.

Step Two

Be sure to address any real-life examples and stories that connect to the list you share with the team. Don't make the mistake of assuming that these problems can't show up in your world. They can! If necessary, get the conversation going by sharing some examples about how these kinds of major obstacles to customer loyalty showed up at another company. People will get the idea.

Step Three

Based on your discussions, come up with some strategies that will prevent these kinds of challenges from sabotaging your efforts to build an emotional connection with your customers.

CHAPTER 15

WHERE THE RUBBER MEETS THE ROAD

It's time to put what you've learned into practice.

What follows in this chapter is an actionable process for creating an experience that customers choose to come back to, again and again. If you've made it this far in the book, you are ready to implement this process. But understand: You can't do this alone.

THE SIX-STEP "I'LL BE BACK" EXPERIENCE DEVELOPMENT PROCESS

The process for creating an amazing "I'll Be Back" customer experience is not just for leaders. It is not just for frontline people, either. And it's not just for people who support customers behind the scenes. It's for everyone in your organization.

This is a series of critical conversations that could take several days and that should, for optimum results, involve multiple people on your team from multiple functional areas. Your best results will come from a diverse group, so if possible, assemble a group that includes leadership and several team members from a variety of departments/workgroups. Choose a person to schedule and lead the meetings and to coordinate the follow-through; the more familiar this person is with this book, the better.

A NEW WAY OF THINKING

Before we start to look at the six steps, consider what it will take to move beyond what we usually do: focus on direct competitors. Many of the teams I work with are already pretty good at comparing themselves and their offerings to those of direct competitors. By direct competitors, I mean the players in our industry who want the same customers we serve and whose customers we want. The process outlined in this chapter is designed to change that way of thinking.

As you will see in a moment, only the second step of this process focuses on direct competitors. We really want to prepare ourselves and our team members to move beyond thinking only about the people in our industry who serve the same kinds of customers and provide the same kinds of solutions that we do. That kind of thinking is simply not enough and, on its own, it's not going to get us where we need to go. The whole purpose of this multi-day brainstorming session is to move beyond comparing ourselves to the competition... because that's only the beginning.

If all you do is copy your competitor, you risk being perceived by the customer as essentially the same as that competitor. You won't position yourself as an organization that's different, and you won't be able to create the kind of unique relationship that turns a repeat customer into a long-term loyal customer.

Many companies, once they realize that the competitor is doing something customers like, simply do the exact same thing, attempting to match what the competition is offering point for point. You do want to understand what your competition is up to, and there are certainly going to be times when it makes strategic sense to emulate them. But don't stop there. Use that as your starting point.

Matching the competition is "baseline thinking." Move beyond the baseline!

Others in your industry are probably also asking themselves, "What are they doing that we aren't?" about you. By focusing your efforts on matching the competition, you risk becoming just another copycat – and in the worst-case scenario, you become a commodity, indistinguishable from the people you are competing with, offering little or no meaningful differentiation for the customer.

To stand out, to secure a major competitive advantage with high levels of customer loyalty, you have to be willing to take it to the next level. You have to up your game. That means being willing to schedule and attend sessions for a team brainstorming process, one that everyone understands must go well beyond the goal of identifying and matching what the competition is doing. I've outlined such a process in this chapter, a powerful one that has delivered great results for my clients.

Before these brainstorming sessions even begin, make sure that everyone planning to attend knows, up front, that the point is not just to understand the competition, but to go beyond the competition. The idea of taking part in this process is to be prepared to look at the very best companies from any industry for inspiration, best practices, and potential game plans.

> # A willingness to look beyond our own industry gives us our best opportunity to create breakthrough levels of customer loyalty. This means setting aside any and all assumptions.

What follows is a series of important questions, and the proper amount of time should be devoted to answering them. Some clients make these questions the theme of a multi-day retreat. It's easy to spend an hour or two just on Step One. Depending on your company, you'll find the right amount of time to get the most benefit. What you don't want to do is lead a short, five-minute discussion around each question. Take the time that you feel is necessary. Even if there is just one idea that improves the experience, that will be time well spent.

Note that, as this process unfolds, it challenges the team to take a close look at the competition (in Step Two), and it highlights what you need to do to get people to say, "Yes, I want to do business with you, and I want to come back and do more."

STEP ONE:
WHY YOU?

This step involves taking a look at your current value proposition – the promise you as a company make to a customer. Ask the members of the team, "Why do people do business with us?" The answer that comes back should tell you a great deal about your company's current value proposition. Beware of long monologues here. Your value proposition should be a brief, easy-to-understand reason why the customer would buy from you, and it should quickly set you apart from other organizations. Answers like, "We have great customer service" are too vague and also something the competition is likely to say. Get the most concise and compelling response you can from the team that reflects the best current answer to the question.

STEP TWO:
CHECK OUT THE COMPETITION

In this step, list out your major direct competitors and then pose two questions for the group, spending significant time on each: "What are we doing that they don't do?" followed by, "What are they doing that we don't do?"

Don't assume that you already know the answers to these questions. Let everyone in your group weigh in and share insights, opinions, and experiences. The answers your group provides to the first question will probably make you feel good about yourself and your company, if you do something different from the competition. The answers to the second question may hurt a little at first, but listen anyway. They will help you find the baseline.

Although you do need to know what your competition is doing, the point of this exercise is that you shouldn't think of that as the end of the discussion.

STEP THREE:
MAKE SURE YOU ARE KEEPING PACE

Based on what you learned in Step Two, you will probably find areas where it's important for you, as an organization, to keep up with or even surpass your competition. As a group, you will want a strategy to take what steps are required to keep pace in the most important area. When you decide that it makes sense to match what someone else is doing, challenge the group to find a way to make that improvement your own. Improve on it or give it a twist. Look for differentiation, not duplication.

STEP FOUR:
MOVE BEYOND YOUR INDUSTRY

Get the same group together for another brainstorming session. Start with the powerful question: "What companies, not including competitors, do you like doing business with the most – and why?"

Take down every name and every reason people offer; create a nice long list. It doesn't matter what type of business your people suggest. If a single team member likes doing business with the company, and can explain why, that company belongs on the list. Popular companies and brands people might mention could include Amazon, Apple, Nordstrom, and Zappos, but there are countless brands recognized for amazing service and customer experience that you may not have heard of yet, so keep an open mind. Some summaries of companies we have already looked at, which drive strong customer loyalty, appear at the end of this chapter; if you want, you can use these summaries as inspiration and examples to get people thinking and talking about the companies they really enjoy doing business with.

Your list doesn't have to feature nationally or internationally known names. It can include a local restaurant, a shoe-repair shop, a local real estate agency, a law firm, a manufacturer, or anyone else a team member likes doing business with, provided that the team member can explain why they like working with that company. Get team members to list out as many specific reasons they enjoy doing business with each company as you possibly can. Everything counts! Write it all down. The more items that show up on this list, the better. Even if a reason seems obvious, or like common sense (such as "They're always nice to deal with") be sure to write it down.

STEP FIVE:
COMPARE YOURSELF AND
BORROW FROM THE BEST

Looking at the list of companies you created in Step Four, make a note of everything they do that you already do. Feel good about this! Invest some time in finding the parallels that highlight best practices you are already committed to.

Next comes the fun part. Look at that list of companies from outside your industry and take as much time as necessary to look for what they do that you don't do. (Trust me: You're going to find some things. If your list from Step Four doesn't point you toward some behaviors and strategies that your company is not currently doing, you haven't completed Step Four properly.) Talk to people on your team who buy from these companies. Use Google. Study their websites. This is your opportunity to find specific best practices that will help you to increase the level of service and experience, ones that are not yet being done by either you or your competition. This is where you will learn how to improve your customer experience... in a way that dramatically sets you apart from the competition.

STEP SIX:
NOW, REVISIT YOUR
VALUE PROPOSITION

Building on everything you've all learned so far, challenge the members of your team to come up with new answers to the question, "Why do people do business with us?"

This was a big question when you asked it in Step One, and it's an even bigger question now. Your goal is to come up with an answer that feels intuitively right to everyone in the room, which everyone in the room can buy into, and which takes your customer experience to the next level.

> **Your aim here is to create a customer experience that is world class, which would be considered excellent both inside and outside your industry.**

Don't be vague. Stay away from general comments like, "We are committed to quality," which are easy for the competition to say they do, too. Focus on what truly makes you different or could make you different. Use this team discussion as a starting point. For instance:

- If you're a restaurant, is there a certain dish your chef prepares that gets rave reviews from customers and has won awards, which no one else in the city offers?

- If you're a hospital, is there a piece of advanced diagnostic equipment that you have that no one else in the area has?

- If you're a manufacturer, is there a product you make and have a patent on, which no one else can create?

You get the idea. Yet, notice that these differentiators are not connected with the way a customer does business with you. Having a patent on a product takes you away from being a commodity, but what if you don't have that to fall back on? If you have an advanced piece of equipment in your hospital, but the experience people have at the front desk doesn't make them feel welcomed and supported, what are you going to do to fix that problem? Look at your process, because that is what will get your customers even more excited. For example:

- As well as offering that special dish that customers love, you give your restaurant's customers access to a page on your website that makes it easy for them to reserve, not just any table, but a specific table, perhaps one that connects to a special memory or offers a view they enjoy coming back to again and again.

- As well as giving your patients access to that cutting-edge technology your hospital has secured, you give all your patients information on how to download a free app that helps them track their diet choices, fitness statistics, and progress toward specific health goals.

- As well as giving your customers access to that patented product no one else can provide, you upgrade your phone system. Now, instead of making customers wait on hold when things get busy, you give them the option of having someone on staff call them back as soon as they become available.

Do you see how these changes create a new level of connection with the customer – by making the process of working with you easier? This is how organizations create world-class customer experiences: they continuously create both product/service differentiation and process differentiation for their customers, and they look beyond their own industry when they're developing ideas in each of these areas. With that in mind, consider using some of the best practices of companies I've shared with you in this book as inspiration for your team's work in Steps Five and Six. Here's a brief recap of just a few of my favorite best practices.

- Create a brief, memorable written statement of purpose or mission, like the Ritz-Carlton Hotel's "We are ladies and gentlemen serving ladies and gentlemen." (Chapter 4)

- Listen carefully to the customer, and make sure you've actually fixed their problem, like Bill Gates of Microsoft did when he took a shift on the customer support line. (Chapter 5)

- Have a carefully worked out system in place for when predictable problems happen, like the St. Louis Blues. (Chapter 6)

- Hire for "nice" first, and train as necessary after that, as suggested by my conversation with Jim Bush, former EVP of World Service at American Express. (Chapter 7)

- Notice familiar customers and engage with them, like Tomas did with me at First Watch restaurant. (Chapter 9)

- Do a little early research to make a customer's experience extra special, like Robin Goodenough did at the Crowne Plaza Hotel. (Chapter 9)

- Find a higher purpose that you believe in and that the customer can believe in too, as was done by Whole Foods, Salesforce, Bombas, ONEHOPE Wine, USA Mortgage, and Keeley Companies. (Chapter 10)

- Give customers more control by creating well-designed self-service options, as done by Wegmans, Costco, and Wal-Mart. (Chapter 11)

- Remove friction from the customer's world, like Barclays Bank did half a century ago when they introduced ATMs and online retailers like Amazon and Zappos are doing today in countless ways. (Chapter 12)

- Every now and then, send customers a handwritten or hand-signed note, like our company does. (Chapter 13)

Congratulations! You've completed Part Two. In the epilogue, I'll share some parting thoughts on getting the most from this book over time.

KEY POINTS

- Copying or matching the competition is "baseline thinking" – meaning it doesn't give you any real competitive advantage. Move beyond the baseline.

- Look beyond your own industry to create breakthrough levels of customer loyalty.

- Companies that create world-class customer experiences continuously develop both product/ service differentiation and process differentiation for their customers.

- Stay away from general comments such as "We are committed to quality," which are easy for the competition to say they do, too.

- Look closely at the best practices of companies featured in this book to help develop your "I'll Be Back" customer experience, and build your list from there.

CONVERSATION STARTERS

- Who should be on the team that participates in the "I'll Be Back" Customer Experience Development discussions?

- Who will lead these discussions?

- When and where should these discussions take place?

TAKE ACTION!

Use the process outlined in this chapter to create a customer experience that is world class... one that would be considered excellent both inside and outside your industry!

I WANT YOU
TO COME BACK

This book is all about inspiring customers to say, "I'll be back." Before we wrap up, I want to inspire *you* to say, "I'll be back."

Yes, I really do want you to return to these pages, as many times as you want and need, while you work to design a customer experience that creates loyalty in your customer base. I didn't design this book to be a one-time read. I designed it to be a guide you can return to again and again, an ongoing resource you can appeal to repeatedly in the never-ending battle to turn first-time customers into repeat customers, and repeat customers into loyal customers.

I know I've shared a lot with you here, and it's only natural to want to come back to a given chapter for a quick refresher of the most important concepts and strategies. I've made that easy for you to do. Start by reviewing the end sections that summarize the key points of each chapter. Then have follow-up discussions based on the conversation starters and action items.

In addition to visiting and revisiting this book, I hope you will also visit www.IllBeBackBook.com. There, you will find easy-to-use, downloadable resources you can share with your team. These resources will help your organization to deepen its emotional connection with customers and make them excited about working with you, continuing to work with you, and referring you to others. Those resources include:

- A workbook you can print out and use as you work your way through the lessons in this book.
- Videos you can use in a team meeting.
- And more!

The more people you share these tools with, the better. Use them within your organization to encourage buy-in to the book's core principles and action items. Use them to start a loyalty revolution!

I hope you'll keep coming back to this book and to all the strategies and tools I've shared with you, in support of that revolution. And as always, I hope you'll tell me about your experiences as you implement the ideas and tactics I've shared with you. I want to hear from you! You can leave a message or contact me at www.Hyken.com.

I'll leave you with one more observation before we say farewell. When you share this book's loyalty-building principles with others in your organization, you may encounter pushback. People may say that you're aiming too high, that you're asking for too much, that your expectations are unrealistic, that internal obstacles in your organization will keep you from putting what I've shared with you into practice. When you hear this kind of response, remember that great things have never been achieved without people being willing to go beyond what is familiar and comfortable. Set the best possible example. Go beyond your comfort zone, and you will inspire others to go beyond theirs. And whenever the opportunity presents itself, share these wise words:

> *"Start wide, expand further, and never look back."*
> Arnold Schwarzenegger

> *"Always be amazing!"*
> Shep Hyken

ACKNOWLEDGMENTS

Without people to read the book, there would be no reason to write one. So, first and foremost, I want to thank you, the reader. I am humbled and honored that you would invest your valuable time in reading this book. Thank you for the confidence you have in my work.

There are some very important people that need to be acknowledged for their help in creating the final product you hold in your hands – or are reading from your screen. Big thanks go to the team at Cara Wordsmith, Ltd, who has done another amazing job in helping me arrange my content and write in a way that is direct and simple to understand. My close friend, whom I often refer to as my big sister, Joan Dietrich, took a hard look at the book. Like her mother, Audrey, who edited my very first book, *Moments of Magic*, Joan found plenty of opportunities to make the book grammatically better. Finally, I'd like to thank the team at Sound Wisdom. This is the fourth book of mine that they have published. David Wildasin and the SW team are amazing.

Finally, I must acknowledge and thank my wife, Cindy Hyken. She continues to support me in my career, encourages me to try new ideas and take risks, and has always been my biggest fan. Thank you, Cindy, for all your love and support!

INDEX

A

C

S

ABOUT THE AUTHOR

"Wow! That company and those people are amazing!"

That's exactly what Shep Hyken wants your customers to say about the experience they have when they do business with your company and interact with your people.

He is the founder and Chief Amazement Officer at Shepard Presentations, where he helps companies build loyal relationships with their customers and employees. He is a customer service and experience expert, an award-winning keynote speaker, and a *New York Times* and *Wall Street Journal* bestselling author.

His articles have appeared in hundreds of publications. He is the author of *Moments of Magic, The Loyal Customer, The Cult of the Customer, The Amazement Revolution, Amaze Every Customer Every Time, Be Amazing or Go Home,* and *The Convenience Revolution.* His wide variety of clients range from smaller companies with less than 50 employees to corporate giants such as American Express, Anheuser-Busch, AT&T, Disney, Enterprise Rent-A-Car, General Motors, Great Clips, Greyhound, Häagen-Dazs, IBM, In-N-Out Burger, Lexus, Marriott, Merrill Lynch, Microsoft, Oracle, Procter & Gamble, SAP, Salesforce, Toyota and many more!

A prolific speaker well-known for his content-rich, entertaining and high-energy presentations, Hyken has been inducted into the National Speakers Hall of Fame for his achievements in the professional speaking industry.

Learn more about Shep Hyken's speaking programs, customer service training programs, virtual presentations and advisory services at

www.Hyken.com.

Connect on LinkedIn: www.Linkedin.com/in/ShepHyken

 @hyken

 ShepHykenSpeaker

 www.ShepTV.com

 @ShepHyken

DON'T FORGET...
THERE'S
MORE!

The REAL value of this book is online!

Go to **www.IllBeBackBook.com** to download the workbook and other bonus content!

And don't forget to follow me:

 ShepHykenSpeaker   ShepHyken   @hyken   ShepHyken   @ShepHyken

ONLINE CUSTOMER SERVICE PROGRAMS

Shep Hyken's best customer service training comes to you in a digital, on demand format. Sharpen your customer service skills wherever and whenever you want with 24/7 access to our online training platform!

The Customer Focus™
Our flagship customer service training program! Your introduction to amazement: The Customer Focus™ walks through Shep's famous cab story and various ways to create an Amazing customer experience by seizing, transforming and improving the moment.

Amaze Every Customer Every Time
Based on Shep's bestselling book of the same name, this program is sorted into five categories — leadership, culture, one-on-one interaction, desire for sustainable competitive advantages and community contribution.

5 Ways to Create an Amazing Customer Experience
Learn how to create an Amazing customer service experience in every single customer interaction, every time.

Six Steps to Create a Customer-Focused Culture
Designed for company leaders and executives, this program teaches how customer service starts at the top, and that leaders are responsible for setting an example for everyone.

How to Manage Angry Customers and Handle Complaints
This program gives organizations complaint resolutions and teaches how to properly deal with angry customers.

Be Amazing or Go Home
Based on Shep's bestselling book of the same name, learn how to be Amazing through the 7 Amazement Habits, containing over 25 tips.

www.ShepardVirtualTraining.com
314-692-2200